BASKETBALL PLAYBOOK 2

ALL-NEW PLAYS FROM THE BEST COACHES IN THE NBA

BOB OCIEPKA
DALE RATERMANN

D1303523

CB

CONTEMPORARY BOOKS

Library of Congress Cataloging-in-Publication Data

Ociepka, Bob, 1948-
    Basketball playbook 2 : all-new plays from the best coaches in the NBA / Bob Ociepka and Dale Raterman[n].
        p.   cm.
    ISBN 0-8092-9870-8
    1. Basketball—Offense.   2. Basketball—Coaching.   3. National Basketball Association.   I. Title: Basketball playbook two.   II. Ratermann, Dale, 1956-
III. Title.
    GV889.O35   2000
    796.323′2—dc21
                                                   99-88336
                                                    CIP

Photo Credits
Pages 2,5: San Antonio Spurs; 8: Miami Heat; 11: Charlotte Hornets; 16, 51, 52: Utah Jazz; 20, 22, 79: Atlanta Hawks; 24: Philadelphia 76ers; 28, 64, 66: Indiana Pacers; 30: Detroit Pistons; 32, 34, 42: New Jersey Nets; 36: Minnesota Timberwolves; 38, 71: Golden State Warriors; 44: Seattle Supersonics; 48, 58: New York Knicks; 68: Phoenix Suns; 73: Orlando Magic

Cover design by Nick Panos
Interior design by Amy Yu Ng
Figure illustrations by Precision Graphics

Published by Contemporary Books
A division of NTC/Contemporary Publishing Group, Inc.
4255 West Touhy Avenue, Lincolnwood (Chicago), Illinois 60712-1975 U.S.A.
Copyright © 2001 by Bob Ociepka and Dale Ratermann
All rights reserved. No part of this book may be reproduced, stored in a retrieval system, or transmitted in any form or by any means, electronic, mechanical, photocopying, recording, or otherwise, without the prior written permission of NTC/Contemporary Publishing Group, Inc.
Printed in the United States of America
International Standard Book Number: 0-8092-9870-8
    03 04 05 06 VL 19 18 17 16 15 14 13 12 11 10 9 8 7 6 5 4 3

CONTENTS

ACKNOWLEDGMENTS

During my time as an assistant coach and scout in the National Basketball Association, I have had the opportunity to work for and learn from eight excellent head basketball coaches. They have provided me with more than an opportunity for employment. They have given me a daily "coaching clinic" on the game of basketball. I have learned from each of them, and these associations have helped me form my philosophy of coaching.

Dick Versace, Bob Hill, Bob Weiss, Bill Fitch, Johnny Davis, Chuck Daly, Alvin Gentry, and Randy Wittman each have helped lay the foundation for my approach to the coaching profession. I also have been fortunate to have the advice, encouragement, and counsel of two of my closest friends, Ed Badger and Will Rey. I want to thank each of these coaches for all he has done for me.

Special Acknowledgments

I would particularly like to thank Alvin Gentry, head coach of the Los Angeles Clippers (former head coach of the Detroit Pistons), who was an inspiration during the writing of this sequel to *Basketball Playbook: Plays from the Pros*. Alvin is a coach who truly cares about his players and assistants. He has proven that he will sacrifice his own interests if it means the people around him will benefit.

And, finally, my utmost gratitude to Anne and Katie for their constant unwavering support and love.

The authors also would like to thank all of the NBA's media relations directors who have contributed photographs, as well as the following people from NTC/Contemporary Publishing Group: Ken Samelson, Rob Taylor, Kristy Grant, and Nick Panos.

—Bob Ociepka

INTRODUCTION

A professional basketball scout has numerous duties. The final scouting report for each team will vary depending on the areas the head coach deems the most important. A typical pro basketball scouting report will have offensive and defensive notes sections indicating tendencies of the opponent, a depth chart listing the roster by position, a call sheet listing the signals for play actions, a personnel section detailing strengths and weaknesses of each player, and a playbook with diagrams of each play.

The one constant from team to team is the playbook section. The pro basketball scout's main job is to study each opponent and build a file detailing offensive actions and "calls" for those actions. In addition to diagramming each play, it is important to indicate which player is the primary focus of the play. These opponents' playbooks have become so large that most teams use computers to store and categorize the information. Typically, pro basketball scouts know the other teams' plays better than their own. Each scout has compiled in his files or computer thousands of plays and actions. As Los Angeles Clippers Head Coach Alvin Gentry has said, "There are no secrets in the NBA." What he means is that every team knows the basic actions and sets of every other team.

This book seeks to expand on the offensive diagrams detailed in *Basketball Playbook* and provide additional actions by categorizing the drawings in a typical scouting format. Most teams catalog their plays according to basic actions such as pick-and-rolls, post-ups, and baseline screening plays. The manner in which a team lists its opponents' playbooks will vary depending on the team. *Basketball Playbook 2: All-New Plays from the Best Coaches in the NBA* provides a sampling of new actions from the following categories:

- Early offense
- Post-ups
- Pick-and-rolls
- Baseline screening plays
- 1-4 Series
- Combination plays
- Specials (with set plays and out-of-bounds actions)

We hope that organizing this playbook this way will make it easier for coaches to select plays they think will help their players and teams take their games to higher levels.

Basketball Playbook was written in 1995 as a result of questions that came from high school and college coaches seeking plays from the National Basketball Association to improve the scoring opportunities and overall play of their top players. That book was an accumulated sampling of NBA offensive plays from official scouting reports and unofficial restaurant napkins alike. The goal was to present some of the common plays used on the professional level that were created to benefit NBA players and raise the level of their games. Those plays were presented in a format that all coaches could easily understand. The message to the coaches was: Even though you don't have a Michael Jordan, Allen Iverson, or Shaquille O'Neal on your team, you do have someone who plays the same position as these pro players. Perhaps your player does things, relatively speaking, at his or her level that would relate to the strategies and plays used on the professional level.

NBA coaches are constantly adjusting, making changes, and using new ideas in an attempt to counter more aggressive defenses. The result of this is many more new plays and actions from veteran coaches seeking innovative ways to utilize their talented players. In addition, since the 1995 season, there have been forty-nine coaching changes in the NBA. New coaches such as Alvin Gentry, Larry Bird, Gregg Popovich, Rick Pitino, and Jeff Van Gundy have brought a wealth of fresh ideas to the game. *All-New Plays from the Best Coaches in the NBA* seeks to describe some of these actions to provide new ideas and inspiration for coaches at all levels. Being able to see the pro plays on paper and then to watch them develop during televised games should aid coaches in putting images together with the Xs and Os.

The plays diagrammed in this book are presented from an NBA scout's viewpoint. The teaching points and areas of emphasis can be determined only by being at a coach's practice session or in his huddle. The information provided with each play should serve as a framework for incorporating the play in a specific system. A good coach is constantly making adjustments and taking what the defense will give. He or she looks to take advantage of switching defenses, traps, and mismatches. There are no secret or magic plays. A good coach can defend a specific play. Basketball is similar to a game of chess. The great coach is constantly tweaking plays to outmaneuver the defense.

As in *Basketball Playbook*, this guide will not identify each play with the specific call used by the coach. The call is the method the coach uses to signal which action he wants his team to run. Coaches will signal their plays both verbally and by using hand signals. It is the job of the scout to decipher these calls to give his team an edge during games and help his team's defense know what is coming. Some coaches are very protective of their calls, although the top scouts will do their best to meet the challenge and identify them. Some coaches will try to hide their calls by covering their faces on verbal calls and by holding out their suit jackets to cover their hand signals. Knowing that some coaches are very protective of their calls, each action in this book will be identified in general terms to describe the play. As coaches add plays to their arsenals, it is up to them to give these plays their own identifying calls.

Positions

To fully understand the diagrams and descriptions in this book, an understanding of basic NBA terminology is necessary. The positions on a team are commonly symbolized with numbers. Here is a brief description of the skills necessary to play each position, along with a list of typical players who fill these positions.

1 = Point Guard

Today's typical NBA point guard is a "scoring point." The players with a pass-first approach (like Jason Kidd) are rare. Point guards have been asked to score more at every level of play. Also, many NBA point guards were shooting guards in college. Because they lack size, they have been converted to play the point.

Keep in mind the type of point guard your team has—one with a scoring mentality or a run-the-show approach.

Examples of point guards are John Stockton, Jason Kidd, Gary Payton, Stephon Marbury, Tim Hardaway, Mark Jackson, Jason Williams, and Rod Strickland. (Note: Allen Iverson, a point guard in size with a scorer's mentality, has been used at the shooting guard position for the Philadelphia '76ers under the direction of Coach Larry Brown.)

2 = Shooting Guard

The 2 position must be able to knock down shots, including on the catch after coming off screens, on spot-ups, and off the dribble. It also helps to have a three-point shooting range. Some shooting guards have post-up skills and can use their size to take smaller 2s to the post. New York got a lot of mileage out of Allen Houston working off the left block in addition to scoring on the perimeter. Shooting guards such as Mitch Richmond and Bryant Stith are also capable of inside-outside games.

Examples of shooting guards are Steve Smith, Ray Allen, Reggie Miller, Kobe Bryant, Eddie Jones, Jerry Stackhouse, Ron Mercer, and Anfernee Hardaway.

3 = Small Forward

The NBA has evolved to the point where, on many teams, the shooting guard and small forward positions are interchangeable. The small forward usually is bigger and typically more of a driver to the basket than the 2. The 3 position also should be a better rebounder and post-up player. In some offenses, the small forward handles the ball and initiates the offense as a "point forward." Scottie Pippen was the best in the business playing this role in the Chicago Bulls' Triangle Offense. The best 3s in the NBA can hit from the perimeter and have the quickness to drive to the basket.

Examples of small forwards are Grant Hill, Jamal Mashburn, Shareef Abdur-Rahim, Glenn Robinson, Glen Rice, Paul Pierce, Vince Carter, and Sean Elliott.

4 = Power Forward

The 4 position is usually a low-post player who is a good rebounder. The power forward is generally the second biggest player in the lineup. If the team has a dominant center, the power forward may be asked to do more of the dirty work such as setting screens, rebounding, focusing on defense, and blocking shots. The more offensive-minded 4s can score in the post and on the perimeter.

Examples of power forwards are Karl Malone, Antonio McDyess, Chris Webber, Shawn Kemp, Tom Gugliotta, Keith Van Horn, Charles Barkley, Mar-cus Camby, and Kevin Garnett (who has also been used at the 3 position).

5 = Center

On most teams, the 5 position is the primary low-post scorer. The best ones cannot be stopped one on one in the post and require a double team. If they can score versus single coverage and pass out to spot up teammates versus post traps, they are invaluable to their teams. Centers who can defend, block shots, and rebound can help their teams even if they do not have good low-post skills. Dominant centers seem to be harder to find, and many teams are employing players at the center spot who would be 4s in previous seasons. However, San Antonio has two great centers, David Robinson and Tim Duncan, and has to use one of them as a 4.

Other examples of centers are Shaquille O'Neal, Alonzo Mourning, Vlade Divac, Dikembe Mutombo, Patrick Ewing, Hakeem Olajuwon, and Rik Smits.

Symbols Used in the Diagrams

To make the diagrams easier to read, a number of court markings have been omitted, except when they are essential to a particular play. Coaches can adjust the plays to fit the court markings of their particular level of competition.

Point guard	1
Shooting guard	2
Small forward	3
Power forward	4
Center	5
Defender	✕
Direction of pass	– – – ▶
Handoff	=
Player's movement	⌒▶
Screen (pick)	⊢
Player with the ball	◯
Dribble	⌇⌇⌇▶
Player has the option of doing one or the other	or

CHAPTER 1

EARLY OFFENSE

Early offense is action that is designed to hit quickly before the defense has a chance to set up. It should flow from one end of the floor to the other and is most often run after a made basket or free throw. The actions detailed in this section are designed to set up early post-up opportunities, get shooters free for shots off single and staggered screens, run pick-and-roll actions on the move, and simply get all five players involved to move the defense.

San Antonio's Early Offense

The San Antonio Spurs utilize a "high-low" system, capitalizing on the talents of their twin towers, David Robinson and Tim Duncan. These players are interchangeable at the 4 and 5 positions, with the first big man down cutting to the low-post and the second filling the high-post spot. With Avery Johnson at the 1 position, pushing the ball up the floor, San Antonio sought to get into its early action quickly in order to get the ball inside before their opponents could set up their double-teaming defense. Jaren Jackson played the 2 position and Sean Elliott the 3 position in the Spurs 1999 championship lineup. A team that has two post-up players that a coach feels can interact with each other from both high- and low-post spots can take advantage of some or all of Coach Gregg Popovich's early system. The focus and continuity of the Spurs' early offense are dictated by the action of the point guard and movement of the ball. This system can be run without calls. Specific actions follow depending on whether the point guard hits the wing and cuts to the ball-side corner, cuts through to the weak side of the floor, drives the ball at the wing or high-post player, or passes the ball from the wing to the corner or from the wing to the high post.

Gregg Popovich

Corner Fill

Position 1 pushes the ball up the floor and passes ahead to 3 filling the right wing. The first big man down the floor (in this case 4) runs to the middle of the lane for a possible early feed from 3 and then posts up on the ball-side block. Player 1 cuts to the corner after the pass to 3. Player 2 fills the left lane, and 5 trails to the high-post position near the top of the key. (See Fig. 1.1a.)

Option 1: Post-feed from 3 to 4.

Option 2: Position 3 passes to 5, and 4 looks to seal his opponent and punch in to the front of the rim for the high-low pass. This is a big action for the Spurs, with Robinson feeding Duncan inside. Remember, the roles of Duncan and Robinson (numbers 4 and 5) can be reversed, as can the actions of 2 and 3, who fill the right and left lanes. (See Fig. 1.1b.)

Option 3: If high-low pass is denied, 5 looks to reverse the ball to 2 and dives hard to the left block. Position 4 spaces out of the lane and occupies a rebounding position off the right block as 2 looks to make a post feed to 5. Players 3 and 1 can spot up at the top and wing to provide spacing and give 5 room to operate in the low post and have a passing lane if the defense double teams inside. (See Fig. 1.2.)

Corner Fill with Dribble Entry

If the wing pass from 1 to 3 is denied, 1 can initiate the corner-fill action with a dribble entry. Position 1 drives the ball at 3, who slides to the corner. The same options shown in Figures 1.1a

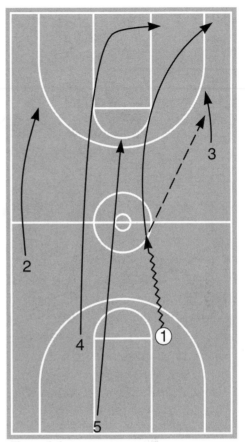

Figure 1.1a.

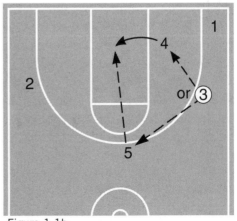

Figure 1.1b.

and 1.2 exist with position 1 playing the wing role. On the pass to the top, the high-low pass is the first look. (See Fig. 1.3.)

Corner Fill with Pick-and-Roll Action

Figure 1.4 shows the early corner-fill action initiated with all rolls reversed except for position 1, who is the primary ball handler. In this case, 1 hits 2 and cuts to the corner. Player 5 posts up on the ball-side block, with 4 in the high-post position and 3 filling the left wing. Instead of feeding the post or beginning the ball reversal option, 3 passes to 1 in the corner. Position 5 steps up to set a back screen for 2, who cuts off 5 while looking for a possible lob pass from 1.

Option 2: Position 5 sets a second screen, this time on the ball for 1 to initiate the corner pick-and-roll option. Position 4 dives to the weak-side block. Position 3 slides toward the top to provide a passing outlet for 1, who also looks for a possible pass to 5 on the roll. The Spurs like to pop Robinson toward the baseline for the short jump shot and catch-and-drive as well as rolling to the basket for a layup.

Option 3: If the pass is made to 3 and a shot is unavailable, 3 can swing to 2, who has cleared to the wing area for a post-feed to 4 on the left block. (See Fig. 1.5 on page 6.)

Guard Through Action

All of the Spurs' early-offense action can be run to either side of the floor.

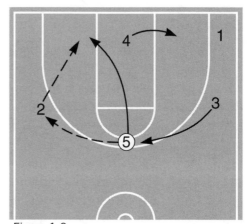

Figure 1.2.

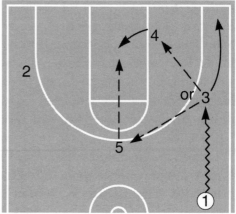

Figure 1.3.

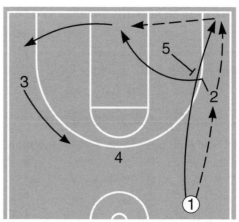

Figure 1.4.

David Robinson

Figure 1.6a shows the offense initiated on the left side, with 1 passing ahead to 2 and cutting through to the weak-side corner. The first big player, in this case 4, cuts to the front of the rim and then to the ball-side low-post position. Instead of holding at the high post, 5 sets a screen for 3 to bring him to the top.

Option 1: Low post-feed to 4.

Option 2: Pass to 3 for a shot or high-low feed to 4. (See Fig. 1.6b.)

If the high-low pass is denied, 3 looks to reverse the ball to 1, who slides up from the corner. Position 5 dives to the right box, and 1 makes the post-feed. (See Fig. 1.7.)

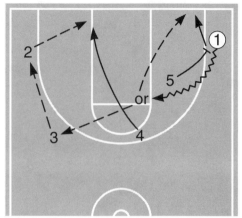

Figure 1.5.

Through with Cross Screen

Player 1 hits 2 and begins through cut toward the weak side. Position 5 cuts to the ball-side low post, and 4 holds at the high post. Position 2 passes to 4, who reverses to 3. Position 1 quickly cuts back across the lane to set a screen for 5. Player 3 makes a post-feed to 5. (See Fig. 1.8.)

This is an action that probably will necessitate a call to alert everyone to the cross-screen option.

High Post Dive Action

The players fill the same positions as in the previous diagrams. Instead of passing to or dribbling at the wing, 1 drives the ball at the player in the high post (in this case, 4). As 1 dribbles toward the top, 4 dives to the left box, trying to establish low-post position. Position 1

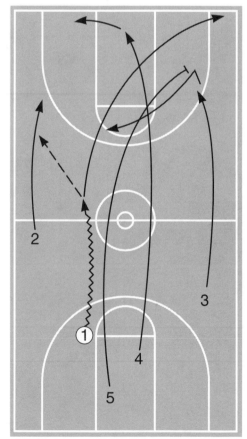

Figure 1.6a.

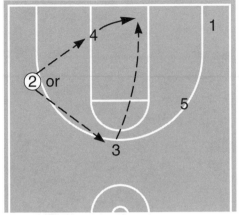

Figure 1.6b.

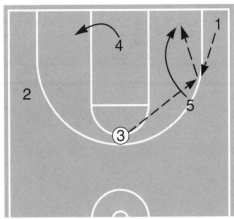

Figure 1.7.

passes to 2 on the wing, who looks to make the post-feed. The dive action by 4 allows him to establish his position on the move, which makes it more difficult to deny him low-post position. Position 5 slides up the lane to occupy his defender and provide another passing option for 2. (See Fig. 1.9.)

Figure 1.10 (on page 9) shows the post-dive action for 5 to the opposite side of the floor, with 3 making the post-feed.

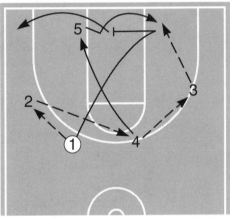

Figure 1.8.

Miami Heat's Early-Offense Series

Miami Heat Head Coach Pat Riley will begin each half running a lot of this early-offense action to get his players moving and also to force the defense to run, move, and defend. The Heat will push the ball into early post-ups, with Alonzo Mourning (5) as the focal point of its inside game. Tim Hardaway (1) will handle the ball and initiate the

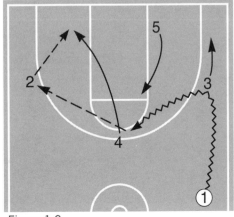

Figure 1.9.

Pat Riley

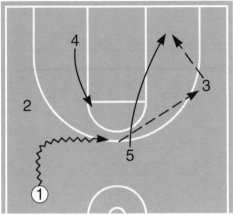

Figure 1.10.

offense. Dan Majerle (2) and Jamal Mashburn (3) are interchangeable on the wings. P. J. Brown (4) operates more on the perimeter than in the post within the Miami system.

Wing Entry to 3 Out–2 In

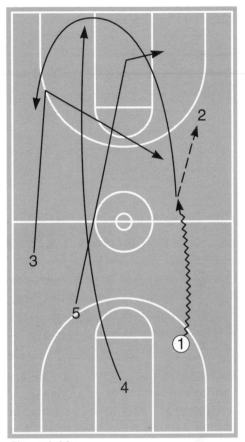

Figure 1.11a.

Position 1 passes ahead to 2 and cuts through to the weak side of the floor. Player 5 cuts to the front of the rim for a possible pass from 2 and then to the ball-side block. Position 3 cuts to the top of the key area from the left wing as 4 dives to the left block. (See Fig. 1.11a.)

Option 1: Post-feed to 5.

Option 2: Position 2 passes to 3 at the top for a reversal to 1. (See Fig. 1.11b.)

The first look for 1 on the reversal is the low post-feed to 4. Since Miami prefers its 4 (Brown) off the box, he will step off the block to set a pick-and-roll with 1 and pop out for a short baseline jump shot. Positions 3

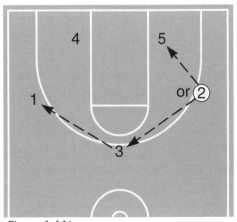

Figure 1.11b.

and 2 slide away to provide perimeter spacing, and 5 punches into the lane for a possible feed from 1.

Note: Brown may hold this low-post position instead of running a pick-and-roll if the post matchup is in his favor. If Mourning occupies the post, he will certainly look to hold his position for the feed inside. (See Fig. 1.12.)

Dribble "Chase" Entry

Miami can begin its early offense with a dribble as well as with a pass. Position 1 can drive the ball to the wing and "chase" the 2 out to the weak side. Positions 1 and 2 now exchange roles. If 4 is the first big player down the floor, he cuts to the ball-side block, and 5 cuts to the opposite post. Position 3 cuts high to fill the top. (See Fig. 1.13.)

Option 1: Position 1 can keep the dribble, looking for 4 in the post. If 4 is not a post-up player, 4 moves out to run a pick-and-roll with 1. Position 5 punches into the lane as the pick-and-roll develops. Players 2 and 3 slide on the perimeter to provide spacing. (See Fig. 1.14.)

Option 2: If player 4 holds the post and the post-feed is denied, player 1 swings the ball to 3. Position 3 reverses the ball to 2, who has been "chased" to the weak side. Player 2 looks to make a post-feed to 5. On the pass to the post, 2 and 3 execute a split (the passer, 2 screens for 3) to occupy their defenders and to provide 5 with a passing option in addition to his own post move. (See Fig. 1.15 on page 12.)

Option 3: On the reversal to 2, 5 has the option of stepping out of the post

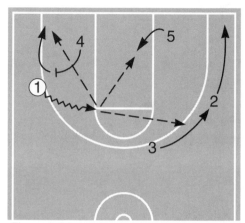

Figure 1.12.

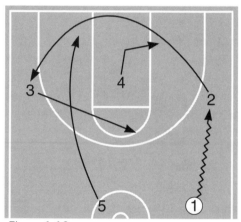

Figure 1.13.

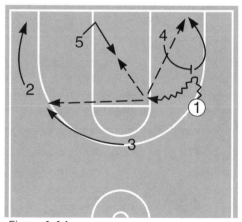

Figure 1.14.

Alonzo Mourning

to run a pick-and-roll with 2. In this case, as 2 and 5 execute the pick-and-roll, 4 punches into the lane, and 3 and 1 slide on the perimeter to provide spacing. The dribble chase option is a good way to run a side pick-and-roll with 2 or 3 without having to run a separate set play. This early action allows the play to develop quickly within the flow of the early offense and helps to prevent the defense from setting up to defend the pick-and-roll. (See Fig. 1.16.)

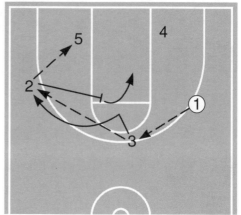

Figure 1.15.

Pinch-Post Action

The pinch-post action is used by Miami to either side of the floor and provides an opportunity for the Heat's 2 or 3 to hit a big player at the elbow and cut off for a quick handoff and drive or flow into a baseline staggered screening action. Depending on who is handling the ball and whether or not the team has initiated the offense with a pass or a dribble chase, any of the three perimeter players can be involved in the different actions.

In Figure 1.17, the pinch-post action is initiated with a dribble chase by 1. Player 3 is chased to the weak side, and 2 cuts high to fill the top. Position 5 cuts to the ball-side post, and 4 cuts to the opposite block but is ready to flash back high toward the elbow. Position 1 passes to 2, who hits 4 cutting to the elbow.

Option 1: Player 4 looks to hit 3 cutting to the basket on a backdoor. (See Fig. 1.18.)

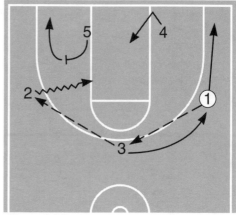

Figure 1.16.

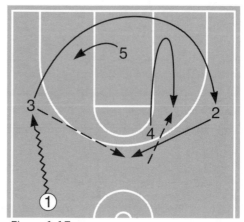

Figure 1.17.

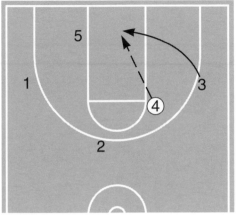

Figure 1.18.

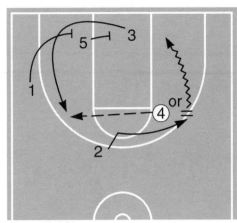

Figure 1.19.

Option 2: Position 2 cuts off 4 for a possible handoff and drive, as 3 continues his backdoor cut and moves off a baseline double screen set by 1 and 5. Position 4 looks to hand the ball to 2 or keeps it and looks to 3 cutting off the double screen. (See Fig. 1.19.)

Option 3: Position 4 keeps the ball and, if his defender has cheated to help on the possible handoff to 2, executes a quick drop step and drives to the basket. If the defense collapses to help, 4 has passing options to 1, who pops back to the corner, to 3, who has cut off the double screen, or to 5, who steps to the open area on the baseline when his defender helps. (See Fig. 1.20.)

If the handoff and pass to 3 are denied, 4 can look back to 2, who has repositioned himself on the right wing for a possible pass. If 4 hits 2, he follows his pass for a side pick-and-roll. As in the previous diagrams, when a pick-and-roll takes place, 5 punches into the lane, and 3 and 1 slide on the perimeter to provide spacing. (See Fig. 1.21.)

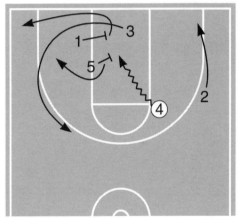

Figure 1.20.

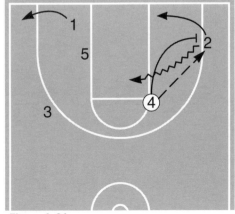

Figure 1.21.

CHAPTER 2

POST-UP ACTIONS

Although there are plays to bring shooters off screens for two- and three-point shots, most coaches prefer that the ball go inside to a posted player. If the ball goes inside to a player who attacks with good back-to-the-basket skills, that player will command a double team that will free the rest of the team for perimeter jump shots. Players can be set up in the post by running hard to the offensive end and establishing their positions as demonstrated in the previous chapter on early offense. This chapter will focus on post ups initiated from cross-screen actions. Before discussing these sets, it is important to look at some of the action by one of the best post-up teams in the NBA, the Utah Jazz.

The Jazz, under Head Coach Jerry Sloan, operate with one of the best post-up players of all time, Karl Malone. He is very difficult to defend one on one in the post, and many teams try to double team him to get the ball out of his hands. What the Jazz do better than any other team is move on the perimeter to occupy the defense and give Malone room to operate. The Jazz also provide him with passing options when the defense runs a second man down to trap him. Coach Sloan demands that his players move after the ball goes inside. They never pass and stand. This allows Malone to take advantage of his outstanding passing skills to free up players like John Stockton, Jeff Hornacek, and Bryon Russell for layups and open jump shots. The Jazz perimeter players move so well without the ball that most teams must double team Malone off the weak side (usually using the defender guarding the 5).

The ball is normally fed to Malone from the wing position. He will catch

Karl Malone

the ball after cutting off a cross screen or back screen, or after a turnout. The following diagrams are not Jazz plays, but they demonstrate the player movement once the ball is passed to the post from the wing position.

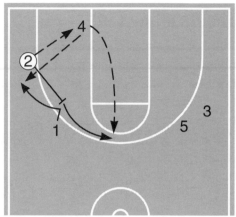

Figure 2.1.

The Split

A triangle is formed on the ball side with 1, 2, and 4. Positions 5 and 3 are lifted out on the weak side. The first action the Jazz will attempt is the "split" of 2 and 1. When 2 feeds the post, he moves to set a screen for 1. If 4 does not have the shot inside, he looks to hit 1, cutting off 2, for the jump shot, or to 2, who pops out after setting the screen. (See Fig. 2.1.)

The Split and Cut

After 2 feeds the post and initiates the split with 1, he attempts to get inside his defender (or 1's initial defender if there is a switch) and cuts to the basket for a pass from 4. When teams attempt to switch this splitting action, Utah usually makes them pay. (See Fig. 2.2.)

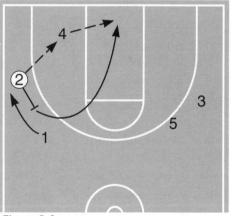

Figure 2.2.

The Split and Backdoor

Again, when teams attempt to switch the split, Utah reads the defense and reacts with quick, sharp cuts. Position 2 feeds the post and moves to screen for 1, who reads the attempted switch and steps toward the screen and backdoors to the basket. Player 2 pops back to provide 4 with a second passing option. John Stockton is especially good at making this backdoor cut. (See Fig. 2.3.)

The Baseline Cut

In this diagram, it is 2 who is reading the possible switch of the 2-1 screen. Position 2 begins his movement to screen for 1 and quickly cuts to the baseline off 4. Position 1 spots up on the wing. Jeff Hornacek and Bryon Russell are adept at this baseline maneuver. (See Fig. 2.4.)

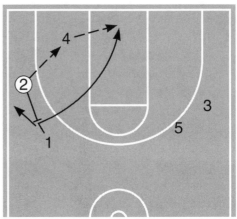
Figure 2.3.

Reading the Double Team Off the 5 Position

As mentioned earlier, because Utah moves so well on its splitting action, most teams will trap the post by sending 5's defender. Figure 2.5a includes the defenders (marked as X) and shows the Jazz movement when this type of double team occurs.

When the ball is fed to Malone, and 2 and 1 execute their split, X5 moves to trap the post. As soon as his defender leaves, the 5 (Greg Ostertag) cuts hard to the front of the rim for a pass from Malone. The only player left on the weak side to cover Ostertag is X3. If he is slow in rotating to cover 5, then the Jazz will have a wide open dunk shot. If he cuts off 5's path to the basket, 3 slides over to a position where Malone can see him so that Malone can make the skip pass out of the post to free up the 3 (usually Bryon Russell) for an open jump shot.

Figure 2.5b displays a cross-screen action used by the Jazz to post Malone and set up the splitting action for Stockton and Hornacek.

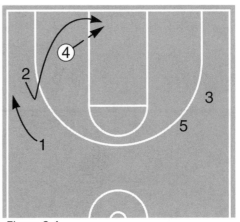
Figure 2.4.

Position 1 dribbles the ball toward the wing, and 2 sets the low cross screen for 4. Positions 3 and 5 are lifted out on the weak side. Position 2 sets the cross and pops back to the ball-side corner. Position 1 hits 2, who makes the post pass, and 2 and 1 execute the split action. (See Fig. 2.5b.)

Atlanta Hawks' Post-and-Split Action

Lenny Wilkens, the winningest coach in NBA history, liked to run a post-up to Dikembe Mutombo for the purpose of freeing up Jim Jackson for a perimeter jump shot. Coach Wilkens tried to eliminate the possibility of the defense switching by having a big man feed the post and set the last screen for Jackson. Most teams do not like to switch when the exchange involves a big and small player.

In Figure 2.6, 1 passes to 4 on the wing and cuts through to the opposite corner. Position 4 feeds 5 in the post and moves to set a screen for 2, who makes the long cut from near the right wing. Player 5 looks to pass out to 2, who cuts high for a two- or three-point shot. Position 4 looks to slip to the rim after setting his screen. If his defender cheats to help on 2, he should be free on the basket cut.

The Hawks would also free up their 2 for his jumper off staggered screens instead of a single screen. In this case, 1 hits 4, who passes to 5 in the post and sets the first screen for 2. Position 4 sets the second staggered screen, and 2 cuts for the perimeter shot. Position 4 looks to slip to the basket after setting the screen. (See Fig. 2.7 on page 21.)

"Moving" Cross Screens to Post-Up

Coach Wilkens would also look to bring either his 4 (Alan Henderson)

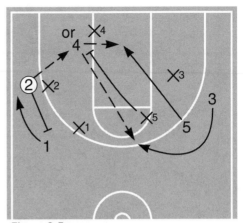

Figure 2.5a.

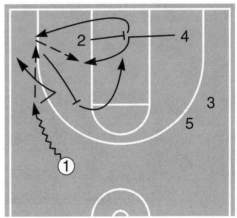

Figure 2.5b.

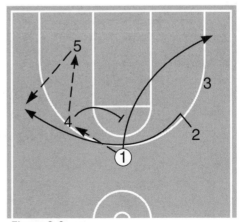

Figure 2.6.

Lenny Wilkens

or 5 (Dikembe Mutombo) into the post off a moving cross screen. The stationary cross screen is easier to defend. The defender will try to put a body on a screener and impede his movement to set a screen. The moving screener is more difficult to slow up, and more fouls will be called on the defense if it is too physical.

In Figure 2.8a, the cross-screen action hits as a misdirection, with the ball being passed to the high post to initiate the play. Position 1 hits 4 and cuts to set a brush screen for 3, who cuts over the top of 1 and across the lane. Position 1 pops back for a pass from 4 as 3 "moves" to set his cross screen on 5. The first option for 1 is the post-feed to 5. His second option is to look to the top for 3, who cuts high off a down screen from 4. This screen-the-screener action gives this play post-up and jump-shot options. Player 2 slides toward the corner to provide spacing.

After time-outs, Atlanta would run the same action, except that it will set a weak-side back screen for 4. The first look for 1 is the lob pass to 4. Position 1 also has the options of passing inside to 5 or hitting 3, who pops out after setting the back screen. (See Fig. 2.8b.)

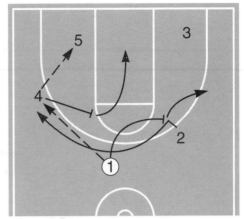

Figure 2.7.

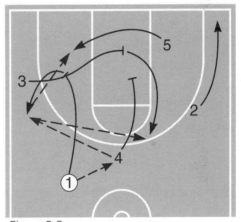

Figure 2.8.a.

Philadelphia's Moving Cross Screen

Coach Larry Brown is one of the best innovators working the sidelines. A scouting report on his team may

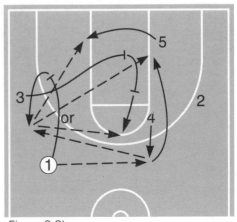

Figure 2.8b.

Alan Henderson

become obsolete before the '76ers next game, as he tinkers and makes adjustments with his offense. Coach Brown will run this play to free either his 4 or 5, looking to get the ball inside to Tyrone Hill, Matt Geiger, or Theo Ratliff. This cross-screening play involves movement and misdirection and is designed to free up 4. Position 1 begins the play by passing the ball to 5 at the top. Player 2 makes a baseline flex cut off 4 into the lane to give the impression that he is the focal point of the play. Position 2 quickly cuts back to set a cross screen for 4. Position 5 reverses the ball to 3. (See Fig. 2.9a.)

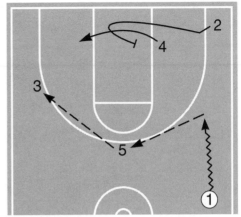

Figure 2.9a.

Position 5 screens away for 1 and works his way to the weak-side board. Player 2 pops out to the corner after setting the screen. Player 3 looks inside for the post-feed to 4 and has the option of hitting 1 at the top if 4 is denied. (See Fig. 2.9b.)

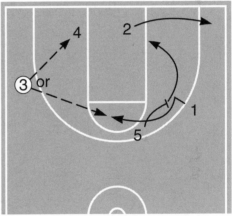

Figure 2.9b.

Philadelphia's Moving Cross Screen with Pick-and-Roll

The same action can develop with 1 and 5 beginning the play with a pick-and-roll. Position 1 dribbles the ball off 5 from the wing to the top, with 2 making the baseline flex cut at the same time. Position 1 passes to 3. Position 2 cuts back to set the cross screen for 4. (See Fig. 2.10a.)

Player 1 spots up at the top, and 5 rolls to the weak-side board as 2 pops

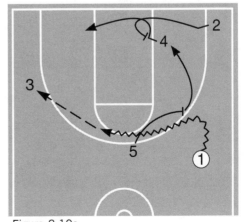

Figure 2.10a.

Larry Brown

out to the corner after setting the
screen. Position 3 feeds 4 in the post,
and, as in the Utah splitting action, 3
can screen for 1 to occupy the defenders and provide 4 with some passing
options. (See Fig. 2.10b.)

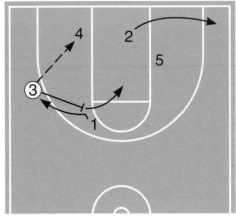

Figure 2.10b.

CHAPTER 3

PICK-AND-ROLL PLAYS

This chapter on pick-and-rolls contains plays that involve secondary actions, although the initial thrust of the play is a screen on the ball.

Detroit Pistons' Step-Up Flare Action

Former coach Alvin Gentry utilized the step-up pick-and-roll to initiate multiple actions. The step-up is a pick-and-roll that is set from the baseline up to the ball, bringing the ball to the sideline side of the screen instead of to the middle of the floor. Many of the Pistons' actions involved 3 handling the ball, as Grant Hill is one of the top point forward players in the NBA and is always dangerous with the ball. In the step-up flare action, Hill handled the ball and helped make the play successful, because the defense had to give help

as he drove off the ball screen. This pick-and-roll involved 3 dribbling off 2. This action involved Grant Hill driving off Jerry Stackhouse. The pick-and-roll takes place at the free-throw line extended. Position 4 aligns to the inside of the left elbow, and 5 is lifted on the weak side, with 1 in the right corner.

Option 1: If 3 can turn the corner off 2's screen and attack the basket, that is all the action needed. If Hill can beat his man the first time the play is run, it sets up the secondary phase of the play. (See Fig. 3.1 on page 29.)

Option 2: If 3 dribbles off 2 and cannot take the ball to the basket, 4 steps over and sets a back screen for 2, who flares off 4 toward the top of the key looking for a skip pass from 3. Position 4 slides to the basket after setting the screen for a possible post-feed. On the catch by 2, 5 sets a down screen for 1. Position 2 looks for his shot and also has the option of passing

Grant Hill

to 1. For the Pistons, Stackhouse can flare for a jump shot or swing the ball to Lindsey Hunter, who has cut off Christian Laettner's down screen. The final option is for Hunter to feed Laettner in the post if his jump shot is not available. (See Fig. 3.2.)

Wing Pick-and-Roll Action

In Figure 3.3a, instead of running a step-up pick-and-roll, 3 passes the ball to 2 and cuts off 2 for a possible hand-off. If the defender on 3 lags, the hand-off and drive may be available. The primary focus of the play, however, is for 2 to keep the ball and pivot to the inside of the floor. Player 4, who again has positioned himself just inside the left elbow, moves to set a quick wing pick-and-roll. Player 4 rolls to the basket, and 5 sets a down screen for 1 just as the pick-and-roll takes place. The timing of the 2-4 pick-and-roll is crucial to the execution of the play. Position 2 looks for his jump shot or passes to 4 on the roll or to 1 cutting off 5.

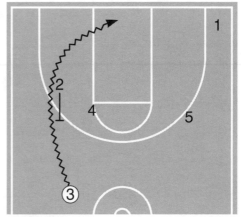

Figure 3.1.

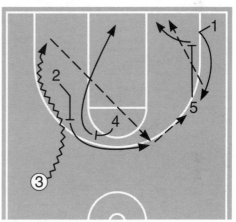

Figure 3.2.

Detroit Pistons' Double Pick-and-Roll Series

Expanding on Doug Collins's double pick-and-roll action, these ideas remained a staple in the Detroit playbook under coach Gentry. Grant Hill, as the ball-handling 3, normally would initiate the play, but the pick-and-roll can be run with 1, 2, or 3 with the weak-side spot-ups adjusted. The key is to run the pick-and-roll off a big man

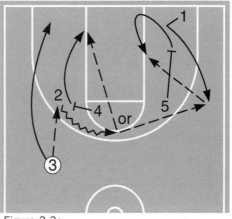

Figure 3.3a.

Alvin Gentry

who can pop out and hit the perimeter jump shot. For coaches Collins and Gentry, it was Terry Mills who could pop out and knock down the outside shot.

The Stacked Double Pick-and-Roll

Position 3 brings the ball up the sideline and prepares to dribble off the double stack set by 4 and 5, who are shoulder to shoulder, facing the sideline with 5 aligned outside the left elbow. Shooters spot up on the weak side so that if their defenders give help, they can spot up for open jump shots. For the Pistons, this is Jerry Stackhouse and Lindsey Hunter. As Player 3 drives off the stack, 5 rolls off 4 to the basket. Player 4 pops out to the wing area. Position 3 looks to turn the corner and gets into the lane for his own play or passes to 5 on the roll, out to 4 for a wing jump shot, or to a spotted 2, if his defender drops to help on the drive. (See Fig. 3.3b.)

The Staggered Double Pick-and-Roll

In this action, 4 aligns on the left elbow and 5 on the right elbow. The action begins with a high cross screen with 4 setting the pick for 5. Position 5 cuts off 4 directly to the wing to set the first of the staggered screens for 3, who has taken the ball down the sideline. Player 5 rolls to the basket, and 3 continues off the second staggered screen from 4, who returns for this ball screen near the left elbow. As in Figure 3.3b, 4 pops to

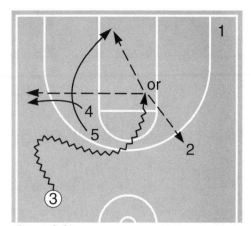

Figure 3.3b.

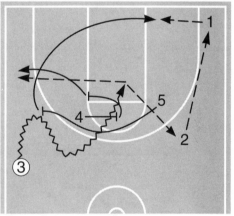

Figure 3.4.

the open area for a possible jump shot, and 3 looks to create his own shot, hit 5 on the roll, pass back to 4, or hit 2 if his defender helps. Position 2 looks for his shot or can pass to 1 in the corner for the low post-feed to 5. Having players cut and move into the pick-and-rolls makes it more difficult for the defenders to provide help. (See Fig. 3.4.)

Paul Silas

Charlotte Hornets' Pick-and-Roll with Back Screen

Charlotte Hornets Head Coach Paul Silas has a great deal of success running a wing pick-and-roll with David Wesley and Elden Campbell. The 1-5 pick-and-roll action initiates the play, but the primary focus is to get a post-up for Campbell. To accomplish this, the 2 (Eddie Jones) aligns on the left block and sets a back screen for 5, who continues his roll off 2 and across the lane to post up on the right block. Player 1 swings the ball to 4, who can feed 5 in the post or pass to 3 in the right corner for the interior pass. (See Fig. 3.5.)

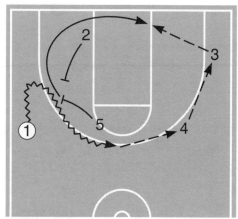

Figure 3.5.

Post-Up Option for 2

This play begins the same way as in figure 3.5 but the focus is to post up the 2 instead of the 5. As the 1-5 pick-and-roll takes place, 2 begins his move to back screen for 5 and then cuts back across the lane to post up on the right block. Player 1 dribbles off 5, who rolls to the baseline, and passes to 4, who again can feed the post himself or swing the ball to 3 in the corner for the inside pass to 2. (See Fig. 3.6.)

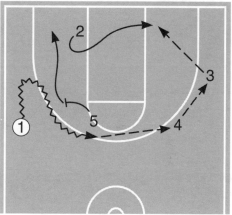

Figure 3.6.

Orlando Magic's Angled Wing Pick-and-Roll

Former Orlando Magic Head Coach Chuck Daly developed the "angled" pick-and-roll to take advantage of teams that try to force the ball toward the sideline or trap it. Orlando ran the pick-and-roll at a forty-five-degree angle, and it was quite successful with Darrell Armstrong (1) driving off the pick from Horace Grant (4). Current Magic coach Doc Rivers continues to use this play with Pat Garrity as his primary screener. If the defender on the ball tries to force the ball away from the screen, Armstrong has a large open area to drive the ball to the basket without help. If the defense tries to trap the

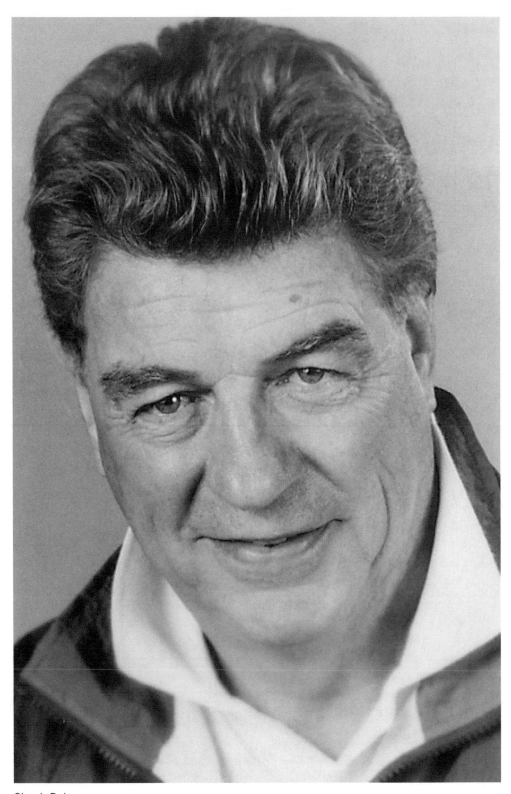

Chuck Daly

pick-and-roll, 4 has an open area in which to pop for a jump shot. The double-screen action on the weak side occupies the defense and eliminates the possibility of a quick rotation to the roll man if the defense traps. The double-down action also provides 1 with another passing outlet if the defense helps off the screener and recovers to his own player. The weak-side double screen sets up a cut for Ron Mercer (2) for a possible jump shot. The key to setting up this play is to have a point guard who is capable of driving the ball to the basket if overplayed and to drive him off a screener who can pop out and hit the perimeter jump shot.

As 1 brings the ball up the sideline, he keeps the ball higher than normal, establishing a forty-five-degree angle with the screener, 4. The 4 steps off the elbow and sets the screen midway between the elbow and the three-point line. On the weak side, 5 and 3 align inside the three-point line and set staggered screens for 2 working off the right block. The stagger occurs as 1 crosses 4 to the middle off the pick-and-roll.

Option 1: Player 1 looks to shoot the jump shot if the defender goes under on the pick-and-roll.

Option 2: Player 1 passes to 4, who pops after setting the screen.

Option 3: Player 1 passes to 5, who slips into the lane after setting the screen for 2.

Option 4: Player 1 passes to 2, who has cut off the double screen. (See Fig. 3.7.)

If the pass is made to 2 and the jump shot is not available, 2 looks to swing

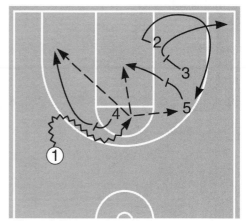

Figure 3.7.

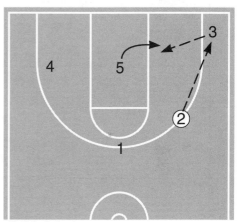

Figure 3.8.

the ball to 3, who pops out to the corner. Position 5 punches into the low post for a possible inside feed. (See Fig. 3.8.)

If the defense tries to force the ball to the sideline or gets caught cheating toward the screen, 1 tries to drive the ball to the outside. The only help available will be from 4's defender, so 4 pops back and spots up for a possible pass and jump shot. If the pass is made to 4, players 5 and 3 double screen for

Flip Saunders

2 as the pass is made to 4. Position 4 looks for his jump shot or the pass to 2. (See Fig. 3.9.)

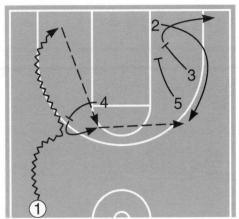

Figure 3.9.

Minnesota's Triple Pick-and-Roll

Minnesota Timberwolves Head Coach Flip Saunders has taken the Detroit stacked double pick-and-roll and added a third screen. This triple action really involves a double stack to a single pick-and-roll. The alignment is different in the Minnesota scheme, with a cleared weak side once the 1 dribbles off the final screen. In this action, 1 handles the ball and drives off the 3-4 double, with 2 spotting up in the ball-side corner. This action involves Terrell Brandon (1) taking the ball off Kevin Garnett (3) and Joe Smith (4). As 1 dribbles off the stack, 3 rolls to the basket and continues to post up on the right box. Position 4 pops and heads toward the top of the key. Position 1 continues his dribble off the single screen set by 5, who rolls to the opposite (left) block. As 1 clears the 5, he looks for his shot or the post-feed to 3. This turns into a good two-man action, with Brandon feeding Garnett in the post. (See Fig. 3.10.)

If the pass to the post is denied, 1 can swing the ball back to 4 at the top for a possible jump shot or a reversal to 2, who cuts toward the wing. This sets up a possible post-feed to 5 on the left block. (See Fig. 3.11.)

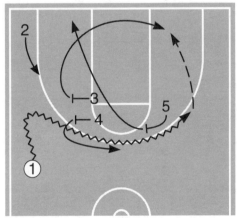

Figure 3.10.

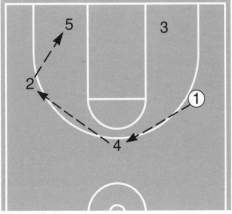

Figure 3.11.

Tim Hardaway

Miami's Pick-and-Roll into Baseline Screening Action

Coach Pat Riley runs a great deal of his offense out of pick-and-rolls, from which the main focus is other action. One of the Heat's more effective actions begins as a wing pick-and-roll with a triple stack formed on the weak side of the floor. Miami will run the pick-and-roll with the 1 (Tim Hardaway) and the 5 (Alonzo Mourning). For the Heat, the 2-3-4 triple stack is typically occupied by Dan Majerle (2), Jamal Mashburn (3), and P. J. Brown (4). The focus of the play is not the pick-and-roll, although Hardaway will not hesitate to take the jump shot or drive if the defense misplays the initial action. Coach Riley seeks to bring his two shooters (Majerle and Mashburn) off baseline screens for jump shots.

Player 1 dribbles the ball down the sideline to the left wing position and dribbles off the ball screen set by 5, who rolls to set a down screen for 2. As 1 dribbles toward the top of the key, 2 cuts off 5, and 3 dips into the lane and cuts off 4 toward the wing.

Option 1: Jump shot for 1, dribbling off the pick-and-roll. (See Fig. 3.12a.)

Option 2: Pass to 2, cutting off 5, for a jump shot, or post feed to 5.

Option 3: Pass to 3, cutting off 4, for a jump shot, or post feed to 4. (See Fig. 3.12b.)

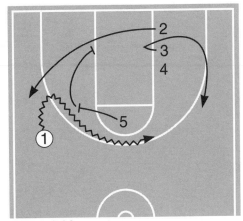

Figure 3.12a.

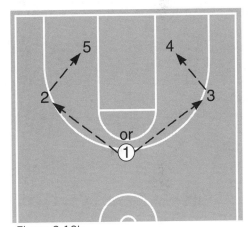

Figure 3.12b.

CHAPTER 4

BASELINE SCREENING PLAYS

Baseline screening plays involve single and staggered screens, and the primary focus is to free up Players 2 and 3 for shots and drives. This section will also include staggered and double screens for the 4 and 5, who can step out and shoot the jumper and back-screen flares for the 1. As in all plays, if there is an opportunity to feed the ball inside after a shooter comes off a screen, that becomes the primary objective.

New Jersey's Loop Action

The typical NBA "Loop" play is most often run as an early-offense action, with teams running into the action after made free throws. The Loop involves bringing a shooter off a set of staggered screens set by the 4 and 5. As shown in Figure 4.1, 2 cuts off 4 and 5 to the top as 1 penetrates to the wing area. Position 3 clears to the ball-side

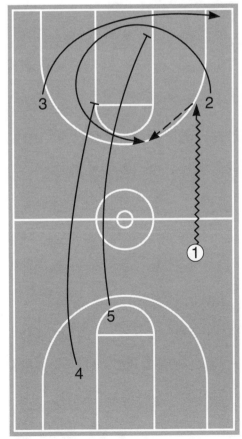

Figure 4.1.

John Calipari

corner to give 2 a clear side for a possible drive if his jump shot is denied.

Former New Jersey Nets Head Coach John Calipari ran his Loop action more as a set play to bring Kendall Gill or Kerry Kittles off staggered screens. The basic difference in the action is that the shooters cut to the ball side of the screens. Kittles and Gill are very adept at using the screens to free themselves for shots and quick drives. If the defense attempts to chase the 2 hard to the top, it gives the offensive player the opportunity for the quick catch-and-drive with a cleared out side of the floor. If the defender takes the short cut and tries to cut off the 2 by moving to the weak side of the screens, 2 has the opportunity to raise up for the jump shot.

Player 1 dribbles to the left side setting up a passing angle to the right high-wing area. As 1 begins his dribble, 2 cuts to the top off the staggered screens set by 5 and 4. Position 3 clears to the ball-side corner. Position 1 hits 2 for the shot or drive. (See Fig. 4.2.)

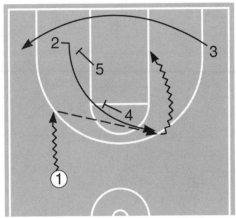

Figure 4.2.

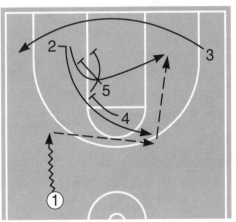

Figure 4.3.

Milwaukee's Loop to Post-Up Action

Milwaukee Bucks Head Coach George Karl has added a post-up focus off the New Jersey Loop play. The Bucks initiate the play in the same manner as the Nets, with the primary focus being Ray Allen cutting off the staggered screens. Milwaukee looks to post up the player who sets the initial screen (in most cases, this will be the 5).

Option 1: As 1 hits 2 at the top, 4, who has set the second screen for 2, now continues into the lane to pick for 5 for the curl back across the lane to the right block. Position 2 looks to make the low post-feed. (See Fig. 4.3.)

Option 2: If 5 is denied in the post, 2 can swing the ball back to 1, who reverses to 3 for the pass inside to 4,

George Karl

who establishes post-up position on the left block. (See Fig. 4.4.)

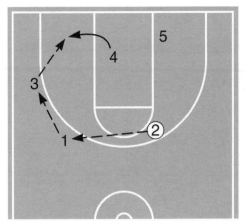

Figure 4.4.

Philadelphia '76ers' Baseline Screening Plays

One of the most successful moves of the 1998–99 season was Coach Larry Brown's lineup adjustment that made Allen Iverson a shooting guard. Although he is a point guard in stature, Iverson has a scorer's mentality in addition to shooting guard skills. The move allowed Iverson to lead the NBA in scoring and help the '76ers reach the NBA Playoffs and advance to the second round.

A good deal of Iverson's scoring came off the following plays that involve his moving off baseline staggered screens. Coach Brown had the luxury of using Eric Snow as his point guard as well as Tony Kukoc to initiate the offense from the 3 position.

In Figure 4.5, the 3 handles and initiates the offense. Iverson, as the 2, cuts off staggered screens set by 1 and 5. Player 1 pops back to the left corner after setting the screen, and 5 holds on the left block. Player 3 hits 2 and cuts off the back screen set by 4.

Option 1: Player 2 looks to throw the lob pass to 3.

Option 2: If the lob pass to 3 is denied, 4 flashes to the ball, and 2 hits 4. This sets up a handoff action with 2 (Iverson) cutting off 4 (Tyrone Hill). Position 2 makes the quick cut off 4 to get the ball back and makes his drive to the basket as 3 clears to the right

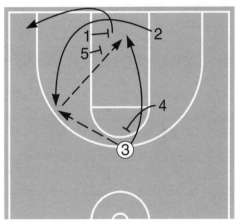

Figure 4.5.

corner. Iverson looks for his path to the basket and can pass out to Kukoc for the corner jump shot if his defender drops to provide help. (See Fig. 4.6.)

Flare-and-Isolation Play

The '76ers can set up the back-screen flare action for Iverson by having him

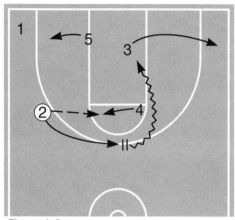

Figure 4.6.

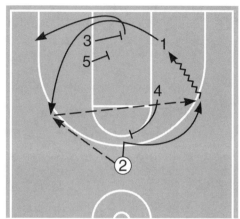

Figure 4.7.

initiate the offense. In Figure 4.7, 2 handles the ball at the top, and 1 cuts off staggered screens set by 3 and 5. Position 3 pops back to the left corner after setting the screen, and 5 holds on the left block. Player 2 hits 1 and flares off the back screen set by 4. Player 1 skips his pass over 4 to 2 for the shot or the isolation and drive.

If 4's defender attempts to step out and help on the flare for 2, 4 can slip to the rim, with 1 making the inside pass. (See Fig. 4.8.)

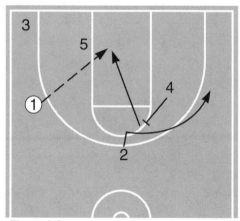

Figure 4.8.

Flare to Pick-and-Roll

Figure 4.9 demonstrates the flare option for Iverson with a pick-and-roll action. If 2 does not have the shot or the isolation path, 4 can follow the pass to 2 and set a wing pick-and-roll. Positions 1 and 3 occupy spot-up positions as the pick-and-roll takes place. Position 4 executes the roll after setting the screen, and 5 punches into the lane.

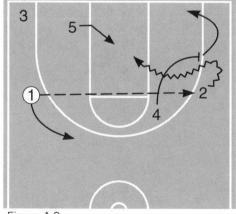

Figure 4.9.

CHAPTER 5

THE 1-4 HIGH-POST SET

Boston Celtics' X Action

When a team prepares to play the Boston Celtics under Head Coach Rick Pitino, it knows that it must be prepared for their pressure defense. In addition, it has to be ready to defend against an offense that involves constant motion. Needless to say, a team has to be in great condition to play this system, and when the Celtics are at their best, they wear teams down on both the defensive and offensive ends of the floor.

A big part of the Boston offense is run out of a high 1-4 alignment. This set allows the 2 and 3 to get a running start into baseline screening action. The players involved in this constant movement are Paul Pierce (2) and Adrian Griffin (3).

The Celtics initiate their cutting action with 2 and 3 aligned on the right and left wings and 4 and 5 at the

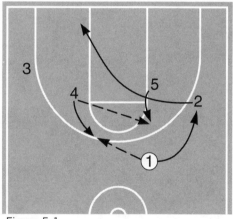

Figure 5.1.

elbows. When 2 is the focus of the play, he cuts off 5, working his way to the left block as the pass is made to 4. Position 1 cuts to the right wing, and 5 pops out for a pass from 4. (See Fig. 5.1)

Position 4 moves to set a down screen for 2, and 3 cuts off 4's back as he moves down the lane. Position 5

Rick Pitino

passes to 2 for the shot or the post-feed to 4, if the pass to 3 slicing into the lane is denied. This action creates a two-man game on the left side of the floor involving Pierce and Antoine Walker (4). (See Fig. 5.2.)

If 5 cannot complete the pass to 2, he passes to 1 on the right wing and follows for a pick-and-roll. As the 1-5 pick-and-roll takes place, 3 cuts to set a back screen on 5. Position 1 drives off the pick looking for his shot—5 on the lob, 4 on the punch into the lane, or on 2 spotting up. This screen-and-roll action for Kenny Anderson and Vitaly Potapenko sets up excellent penetration and draw-and-kick possibilities. (See Fig. 5.3.)

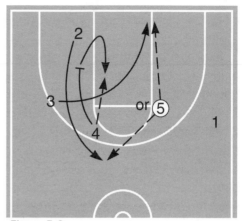

Figure 5.2.

Boston Celtics' Post-Drop Action

From the 1-4 high alignment, Coach Pitino will cut Pierce (playing the 3 spot) to a post-up from the left wing. Position 1 hits 4 at the left elbow and cuts to the left wing. Position 3 makes a hard basket cut for a possible back-door pass and, if this is denied, looks to seal his defender and cut back to post up on the left block. Player 4 makes the post-feed to 3. (See Fig. 5.4.)

Down-Screen Option: Again, there are no passing and standing in the Celtics' offense. If the inside pass from 4 to 3 is denied, 4 looks to reverse the ball to 2, who cuts to the top off a screen from 5. Position 4 sets a down screen for 3, who cuts toward the

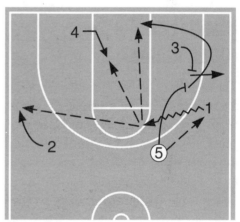

Figure 5.3.

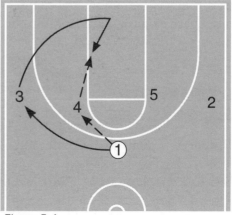

Figure 5.4.

elbow for the pass from 2 and the jump shot. (See Fig. 5.5.)

Back-Screen Option: A very effective option for Boston, if the interior pass is denied, is for 4 to reverse the ball to 2, who has cut off 5's screen and cut off a back screen set by 3. For the Celtics, this involves Pierce setting the screen for Walker. Player 2 looks for the lob pass to a cutting 4. If the player guarding 3 looks to help on the lob, 3 should be free for the jump shot as he pops to the top. (See Fig. 5.6.)

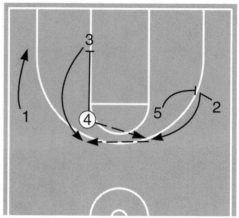

Figure 5.5.

Utah Jazz's 1-4 Set (UCLA Action)

The Utah Jazz, under Head Coach Jerry Sloan, has been the NBA's top team in terms of execution over the last several years. Utah has been known for its low-post game featuring Karl Malone and its side pick-and-rolls with Malone and John Stockton. Utah also is especially adept at running its offense out of the UCLA set or 1-4 high set. The UCLA action involves a wing pass and cut off the high post. There are, of course, numerous options and counters that Coach Sloan has incorporated into this set.

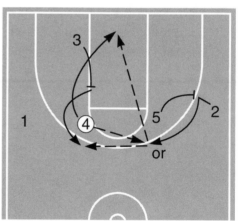

Figure 5.6.

UCLA to Baseline Staggered Screens

Option 1: From the 1-4 high alignment, 1 begins the play with a wing pass to 2 (Stockton to Jeff Hornacek). After the pass, 1 makes a "UCLA cut" off 4 toward the right block. Position 1 can cut inside or outside of 4, depending on the path taken by his defender. The 4 cannot move, so it is the job of the 1 to run his defender off the wide screen set by 4. As the 4 (Karl Malone) sets a wide screen, Stockton will get at least one or two layups a game off

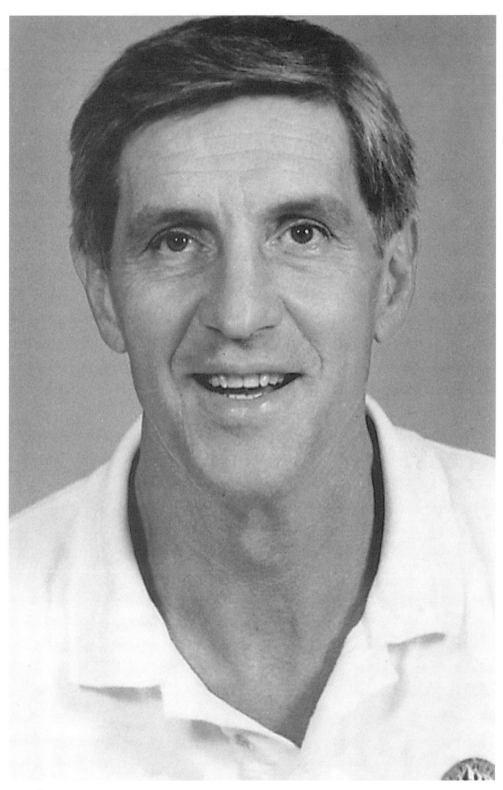

Jerry Sloan

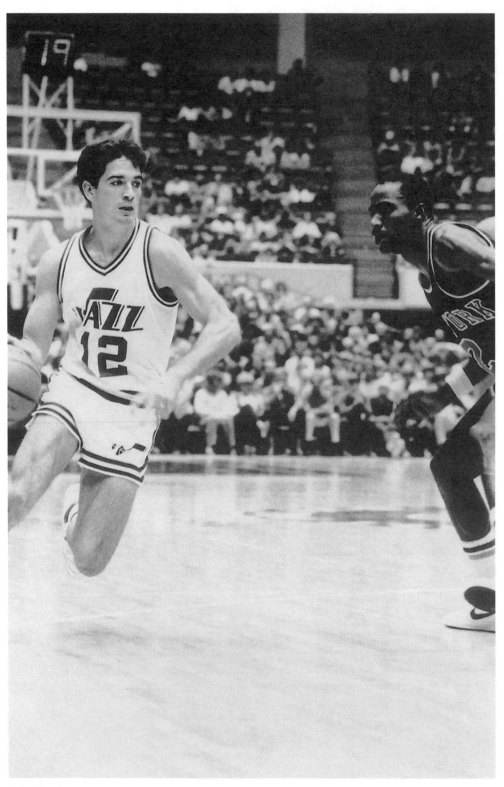

John Stockton

this cut and return pass from 2. (See Fig. 5.7.)

Option 2: The 4 pops back after 1 makes his cut. If the layup pass is denied, 2 hits 4. If the defender on 4 drops to help on 1, 4 should be open for a jump shot. If no shot is available, the secondary part of the play develops. Positions 3 (Bryon Russell) and 5 (Greg Ostertag) drop from the left wing and elbow to set baseline staggered screens for 1. Position 4 looks to hit 1 cutting off the screens. A second passing option is available to 4 as 3 cuts to the right block after screening for 1. If the defender on 3 helps on 1, or if there is some confusion on a switch, 3 will be open inside. (See Fig. 5.8.)

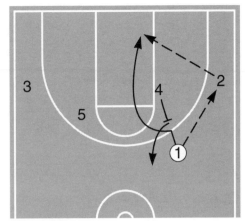

Figure 5.7.

UCLA to Back Screen

From the same 1-4 alignment, the Jazz will run a back-screen option, with Stockton setting a pick for Malone. As in the initial set, 1 hits 2 and makes a UCLA cut off 4 to the right block. Instead of cutting off the weak side, 1 cuts back up the lane and sets a back screen on 4's defender. Position 4 cuts to the post as 1 pops high. Position 2 looks to make the post-feed to 4. (See Fig. 5.9.)

If this pass is denied, 2 can hit 1 at the top for the shot or the high-low feed to 4. (See Fig. 5.10.)

Dribble-Entry Option to Back Screen

If the pass from 1 to 2 is denied, 1 can initiate the play with a dribble entry. Position 1 drives the ball at 2 on the

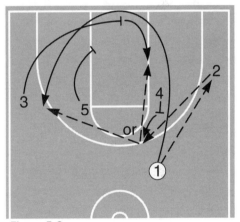

Figure 5.8.

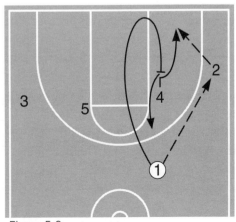

Figure 5.9.

wing and takes his position. Player 2 cuts to the right block and up the lane to set the back screen for 4, taking the role of the 1. Player 4 cuts off 2 to the post, and 2 pops high. Player 1 looks to feed 4 in the post or 2 at the top. (See Fig. 5.11.)

UCLA Set to Pick-the-Picker Action

This action takes place on the left side of the floor so that the initial screen will bring the 4 (Karl Malone) to a post-up position on the left block as the first option. From the same 1-4 alignment, 1 hits 3 on the wing and makes a UCLA cut toward the left block, with the primary option being to set a back screen for 4. Player 1 quickly cuts across the lane to set the pick. Player 3 looks inside to 4 for the post feed or to the top for 1, who cuts off a screen from 5, completing the pick-the-picker action. (See Fig. 5.12.)

Dribble Entry to Pick-the-Picker Action

Utah will also switch the positions of the 2 and 3 when this play is called so that it can involve both Stockton and Hornacek in this action, especially if a dribble entry is used. If the pass from 1 to 2 is denied, or if Stockton wants to look for the Hornacek jump shot off the top, he will dribble the ball at 2 on the wing. Position 2 now assumes the

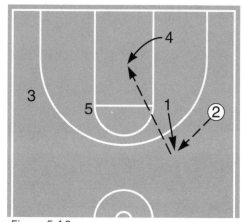

Figure 5.10.

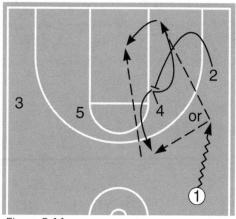

Figure 5.11.

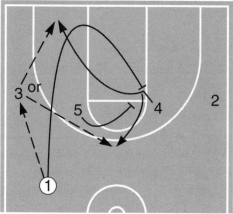

Figure 5.12.

role of the 1 and sets the back screen for 4. Position 2 cuts to the top off 5 on the pick-the-picker action. The 1 has the option of the post-feed to 4 or the pass to 2 at the top for the jump shot. (See Fig. 5.13.)

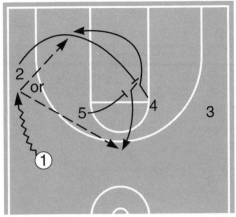

Figure 5.13.

CHAPTER 6

COMBINATION PLAYS

The plays in this chapter are hard to categorize because they evolve from and include a variety of actions. These plays begin with zipper action, Hawk cuts, and box sets. The end result of these plays may be a pick-and-roll, staggered screens for a jump shot, or a low post-feed. The greatest strength of combination plays is their versatility. They include multiple options and generally involve scoring options for all five players.

New York Knicks' Zipper-to-Baseline Triple

New York Knicks Head Coach Jeff Van Gundy got a lot of mileage out of this play in leading his team to the 1999 NBA Finals. This zipper action uses the

skills of his top players and contains multiple options that make it very effective. The zipper screen (which involves a down screen moving from the ball-side elbow for a player positioned on the ball-side block) brings Allan Houston (2) to the top off Patrick Ewing (5). When Latrell Sprewell is used as the 2, he is the player who cuts high off 5. This frees up a very skilled isolation player for a one-on-one play or pick-and-roll action off the top while the New York point guards (Charlie Ward or Chris Childs) run off triple baseline staggered screens.

Basic Set

Position 1 dribbles the ball to the wing as 2 zippers to the top off the down screen from 5. Player 1 hits 2 and cuts off the triple baseline staggered screens

Jeff Van Gundy

set by 5, 3 (set in front of the rim), and 4 (set off the left block). The 2 adjusts his position with a dribble to improve his passing angle and looks to pass to 1. Player 4 posts up after setting the last screen, and 1 has the option of a shot or post-feed. (See Fig. 6.1.)

The 4 also has the option of stepping out of the post and running a wing pick-and-roll with 1 after the ball has been reversed. (See Fig. 6.2.)

After 3 sets the second screen for 1, he clears the lane by cutting off 5 on the right side. Player 2 now has the option of looking back to 3 if 1 is denied. For New York, this involves a pass from Houston to Sprewell. (See Fig. 6.3.)

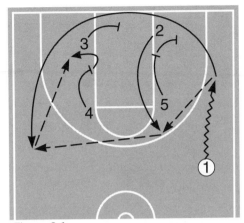

Figure 6.1.

Baseline Counter for 1

As soon as 1 anticipates that his defender is cheating over the top to try to beat him to the weak side off the triple, he can run the counter. On the counter, he cuts just below the back screen from 5 and cuts back toward the right corner. If 5 has the opportunity to set a legal screen, he can pick 1's defender. The 2 hits 1 popping back for the shot or post-feed to 5. New York likes to pop Ward back to set up the post-feed to Ewing. (See Fig. 6.4.)

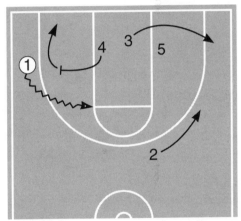

Figure 6.2.

Baseline Counter to Pick-and-Roll

The Knicks will run the counter action with 2 passing to 1 after he pops back. Instead of holding the post, 5 will step

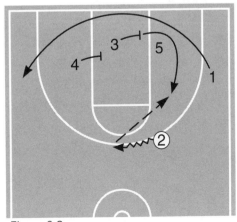

Figure 6.3.

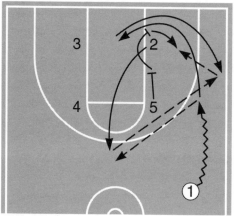

Figure 6.4.

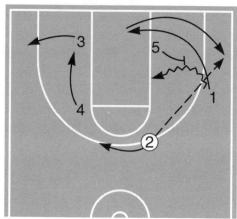

Figure 6.5.

out to run pick-and-roll action with 1. (See Fig. 6.5.)

One-on-One Action for the 2

When Allan Houston is matched with a defender whom he can attack off the dribble, New York will give him the green light to attack off the top. Houston's teammates read his action and provide him with the spacing he needs, instead of running the baseline triple. Figure 6.6 shows the zipper action with 2 cutting high off 5. Position 1 pops back off 5 as in the countermove. Position 3 cuts to the left corner, and 4 flattens out to the left block. This provides 2 with spacing to drive, and it resembles a 1-4 low set. (See Fig. 6.7.)

Elbow Pick-and-Roll Action

The final option off this set involves an elbow pick-and-roll with Houston and Ewing. The 1 dribbles to the wing and hits 2, who zippers to the top off 5.

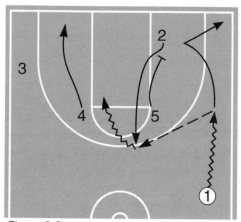

Figure 6.6.

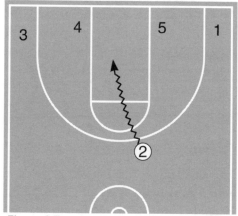

Figure 6.7.

Position 1 runs the baseline off the triple staggered screens, as shown in the basic set. Position 2 ignores 1 as 5 steps up from the baseline to run an elbow screen with 2. Ewing will normally pop for a jump shot as 2 has a clear side of the floor to operate. Player 3 pops back to the left corner, and 4 holds on the left block. (See Fig. 6.8.)

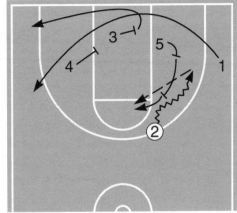

Figure 6.8.

Atlanta Hawks' Zipper to Cross Screen

This action has been run successfully by a number of coaches but most recently by Lenny Wilkens in Atlanta.

This play begins with a 5-3 zipper screen as 1 dribbles the ball to the right-wing area. Player 1 passes to 3 at the top. As 3 catches the ball, 2 sets a back screen for 4. Position 4 cuts toward the rim for a possible lob pass, and 2 pops out after setting the pick. This involves a possible lob to Alan Henderson or a pass to Jim Jackson for a possible jump shot. (See Fig. 6.9.)

If the pass is made to 2 and the shot is not available, 4 continues off his cut to set a cross screen for 5. The action is designed to move quickly so that it turns into a pick-the-picker play, with 5 setting a down screen for 3 and then receiving a cross screen from 4. Often NBA teams will switch a screen that involves one big man screening for another. If this is the case, the 4 must attempt to seal the defender who switches on to him and roll back to the ball. The 2 now has the passing options

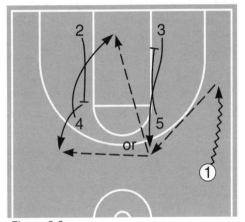

Figure 6.9.

of feeding 5 cutting to the post or 4 on the roll back. The primary focus of this action is Dikembe Mutombo (5) in the post. (See Fig. 6.10.)

Minnesota's Hawk Combination Play

Coach Flip Saunders uses a set in Minnesota that features Kevin Garnett working off the right box, evolving into numerous options. The initial thrust of the play is a Garnett post-up. (See Fig. 6.11.) If he is denied inside, he can cut up the lane to set a "moving Hawk screen." (The typical Hawk cut involves a player moving on an angle from the weak to the ball side of the floor off a stationary screen.) The Wolves use this action with the 3 moving to set a back screen for the 2. The 2 cuts off 3 and continues through the lane and off a weak-side double screen from 4 and 5. For the Wolves, this means that Malik Sealy (2) is cutting off the double screen set by Joe Smith (4) and Dean Garrett (5). After setting the back screen, 3 cuts to the right wing to execute a pick-and-roll with 1. This Terrell Brandon-Kevin Garnett pick-and-roll is the key to the play. Brandon drives hard off the screen looking to get into the lane for his jump shot as the first option. Garnett pops out toward the right baseline for a possible pass from Brandon as the second option. This often sets up a very effective isolation play for Garnett. The weak-side double for 2 gives the 1 an additional passing option, and Sealy is a good shooter cutting off screens. Player 4 will slice over the top of 5 after setting the double, giving 1 an additional passing option. (See Fig. 6.12.)

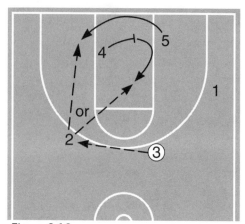

Figure 6.10.

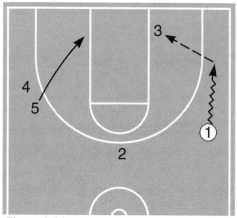

Figure 6.11.

Minnesota's "Hawk Action" with Counter

Minnesota will use a counter to this basic set that involves bringing Garnett

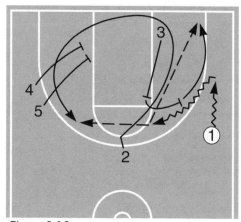

Figure 6.12.

off a second set of double screens. The play begins in the same manner with a 3-2 back screen. The 2 cuts off the weak-side double screen, and 1 and 3 run a side pick-and-roll.

Instead of looking for his own shot, 1 completes the pass to 2. Player 3 rolls toward the basket and continues across the lane, cutting off a second double screen set by 4 and 5. Player 2 swings the ball to 3 cutting to the post. Player 4 cuts off 5 into the lane to complete the action. (See Fig. 6.13.)

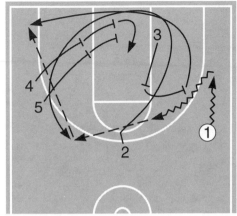

Figure 6.13.

Minnesota's Traditional "Hawk" to Pick-and-Roll

A similar action is run by the Wolves off the left side with the traditional Hawk set. In this action, 2 cuts off a stationary 4, who aligns in the high post. Position 2 continues across the lane and off staggered screens set by 3 and 5. Position 4 cuts to the wing for a pick-and-roll with 1, who looks for the pass to 2. (See Fig. 6.14.)

The focus of this play is the 4. He continues his roll across the lane and cuts off a second set of staggered screens from 3 and 5. The 2 looks to feed 4 cutting to the post or off the block toward the short corner. (See Fig. 6.15.)

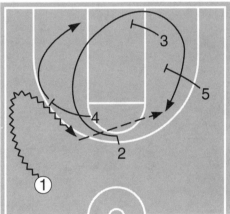

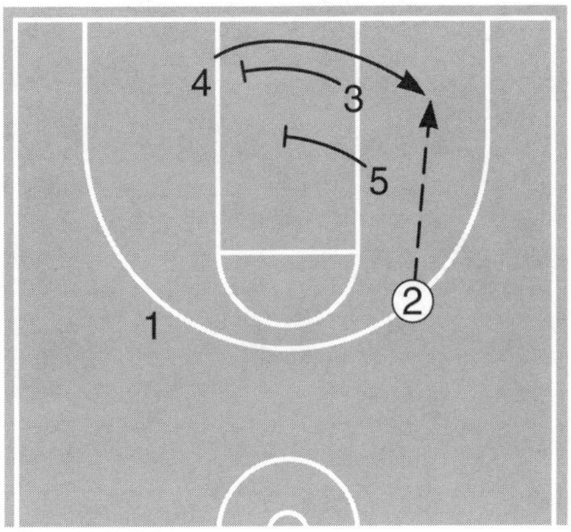

Figure 6.14.

Indiana's Box Set

The Indiana Pacers, under 1997–98 NBA Coach of the Year Larry Bird, used

Figure 6.15.

Larry Bird

the box set to generate scoring opportunities for Reggie Miller (2) and Jalen Rose (3) off baseline screens. In turn, the ability of Miller and Rose to shoot the ball sets up post opportunities for Rik Smits (5) and Dale Davis (4). The box set is a 1-2-2 look, with 4 and 5 aligned in the high post at the elbows and 2 and 3 on the low blocks. This combination play zeros in on either shooter, depending on the direction the 1 (Mark Jackson) takes his dribble.

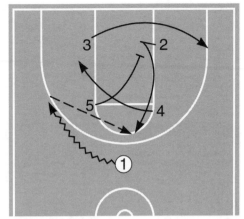

Figure 6.16.

From the box set, 1 dribbles the ball to the left wing to initiate the initial thrust of the play for the 2. As 1 dribbles past 5, 5 and 4 begin an X move in the high post. Players 5 and 4 make this high cross, with 4 cutting to the left block and 5 setting a down screen for 2. The first option is to look for the post-feed to 4. The second option is to pass to 2 cutting to the top off 5. The 3 times his cut to move off 5 out to the right corner as 5 posts up on the right block. (See Fig. 6.16.)

If the pass is made to 2 at the top and he is not free for the shot, he swings the ball to 3, who looks to make the low post-feed to 5. (See Fig. 6.17.)

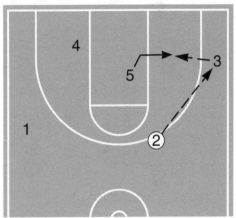

Figure 6.17.

Coach Bird ran this action specifically looking to reverse the ball to post up Smits on the right block.

Figure 6.18 shows the same action run to the opposite side of the floor. For the Pacers, this means that Smits will cut to the right block for the initial post look off the high X action, and the 4 will set a down screen to bring Mullin to the top. Position 2 cuts off 4 to the left corner. The same options exist.

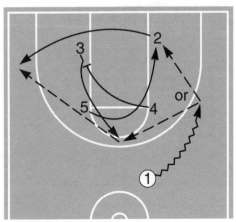

Figure 6.18.

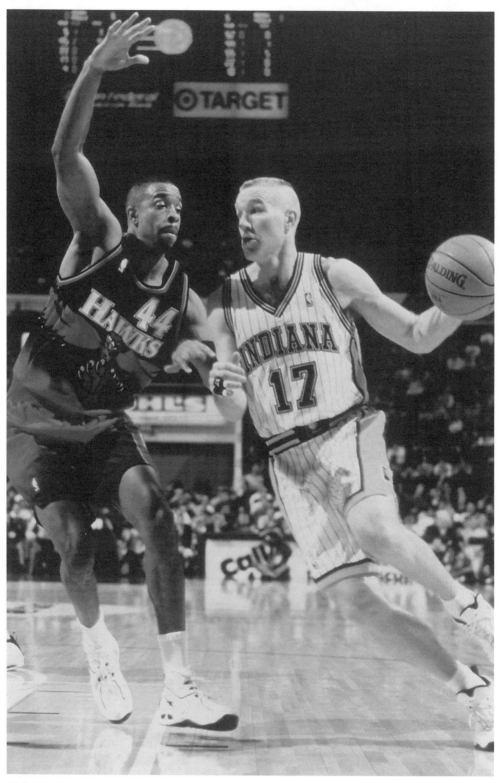

Chris Mullin

CHAPTER 7

SIDE OUT-OF-BOUNDS PLAYS

Phoenix's Slice Action

The Phoenix Suns, under former Head Coach Danny Ainge, ran a side out-of-bounds play that is one of the most difficult in the NBA to defend. The basic action gets the ball into the hands of Jason Kidd (1). With the ball in the hands of one of the best point guards in the NBA, Penny Hardaway (2) makes a slice cut off a strong low-post player, usually Tom Gugliotta (4). This sets up an action that makes giving help a virtual impossibility.

Position 2 inbounds the ball, with 1 aligned at the ball-side elbow and 4 at the ball-side block. Positions 3 and 5 are lifted out on the weak side. The 1 pops out to receive the inbounds pass, and 2 makes a hard slice cut into the lane over the top of 4. Player 1 looks to hit 2 cutting into the lane if his defender gets caught on the screen from 4. Player 4 punches into the lane and looks for the low post-feed from 1. If the defender guarding 4 helps on 2, he should be able to seal his man and free himself for the post-feed. (See Fig. 7.1.)

If the defense does a good job and denies the cut by 2 and the post-up from 4, the second phase of the play begins, with 2 cutting back off a down screen from 4. Normally, the defender on 2 has worked very hard to defend the cut and is vulnerable to be screened.

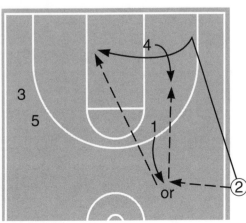

Figure 7.1.

Danny Ainge

Figure 7.2.

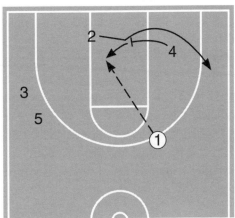

Figure 7.3.

In this case, 1 looks to pass to 2 cutting off 4 for the jump shot or the low post-feed. (See Fig. 7.2.)

The Suns have used Hardaway cutting off this screen to knock down jump shots.

When executing the 4-2 down screen, Gugliotta is very active at slipping the screen. If the defender on 4 begins to cheat out to help on 2, 4 slips to the rim for the pass from 1. (See Fig. 7.3.)

When the defender guarding the 2 begins to cheat out on the screen, 2 fakes cutting off 4 and backdoors to the rim. (See Fig. 7.4.)

To give the play a different look and to help ensure that the inbounds pass can be made to 1, the play can begin with a down screen. In this case, 4 begins at the ball-side elbow, and 1 aligns at the ball-side block. The 1 makes a zipper cut off the down screen from 4 for the pass from 2. The ball is again in the hands of 1, and the slice play with all options is once again set up. (See Fig. 7.5a.)

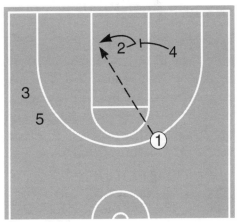

Figure 7.4.

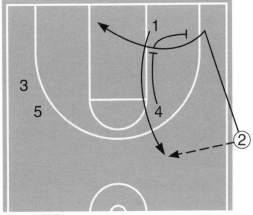

Figure 7.5a.

Players 3 and 5 are generally in a lifted position and not involved in the play. If a three-point shot is needed, or if 1 cannot hit 2 or 4, he looks for a pass to 3. Player 3 dips below 5 and quickly cuts back off 5's screen for a possible three-point shot. (See Fig. 7.5b.) The Suns' Rodney Rogers, an excellent long-range shooter, is often the beneficiary of this action.

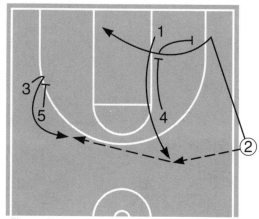

Figure 7.5b.

Los Angeles Lakers' Triangle Post-Up Play

The Lakers Head Coach Phil Jackson will set up in their triangle alignment on side out-of-bounds plays. The primary focus is to post up Shaquille O'Neal. Player 3 inbounds the ball and hits 2 at the top of the triangle. Player 3 slices off 5 to the weak-side wing, and 1 cuts on the right side for the pass from 2. (See Fig. 7.6a.)

Player 1 makes the post-feed to 5 and sets a high split screen on 2 and then a diagonal down screen for 4. Player 5 looks for his shot or pass to 2 or 4 cutting off screens. (See Fig. 7.6b.)

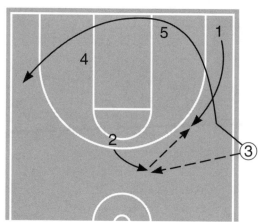

Figure 7.6a.

New York Knicks' Pick-the-Picker (for a Three-Point Shot)

Coach Jeff Van Gundy has used this play late in games when in need of a three-pointer. He will adjust his lineup to include all three-point shooters,

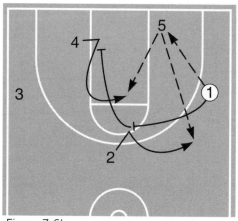

Figure 7.6b.

Latrell Sprewell

except for the 5 (Patrick Ewing). A late game situation for the Knicks will usually include a lineup of Charlie Ward (1), Chris Childs (2), Allan Houston (3), and Latrell Sprewell (4).

The play begins with 1 setting a back screen for 3. Position 1 then cuts high off a screen from 5 (pick-the-picker action) for the inbounds pass from 2. (See Fig. 7.7.)

After passing to 1, 2 steps in to set a down screen for 3. With the proper timing, 3 has cut off staggered screens from 1 and 2. The 2 pops back to the corner, behind the three-point line. The 4 occupies the defense on the weak side and cuts high behind the three-point line, looking for a possible pass from 1 if 3 is denied. Player 1 looks for the three-point shot as the first option, then to 3. If 3 cannot get a shot, he looks to 2 spotting up in the corner. (See Fig. 7.8.)

at the left elbow. Player 1 cuts through to the corner, and 4 pops out to receive the inbounds pass from 3. As 4 receives the pass, 5 sets an angle down screen for 2, who begins the play directly in front of the rim. Player 4 passes to 2

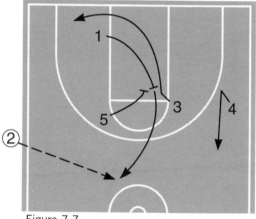
Figure 7.7.

Coach Chuck Daly's Hook Play

The hook side out-of-bounds play has been part of Coach Chuck Daly's arsenal since his days as coach of the Detroit Pistons. He can run the play to produce a jump shot or a post-up for his 2. For his most recent team, this meant a scoring opportunity for either Penny Hardaway or Nick Anderson. In the "old days," it resulted in a Joe Dumars jumper.

The hook action begins with 1, who starts at the top of the key, making a Hawk-type cut off 4, who is aligned

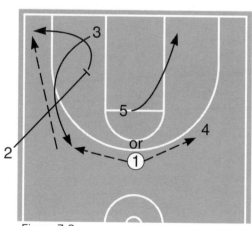
Figure 7.8.

Nick Anderson

for the shot or post-feed to 5. (See Fig. 7.9.)

The hold option (for a post-up) occurs out of the same set and begins with the same initial action. The difference is that when 4 receives the inbounds pass, 5 decoys a down screen and pops out for a pass from 4. Position 2 cuts to the right block for a post-feed from 5. Position 5 passes inside and cuts through to the opposite block to clear his defender through and to establish weak-side rebounding position. (See Fig. 7.10.)

The hold option (for an isolation) is run exactly the same way except that 2 cuts out toward the wing for the pass from 5. If Hardaway feels he has a better scoring opportunity by moving away from the basket and then taking his defender off the dribble in an isolation, he will use this maneuver. (See Fig. 7.11.)

Philadelphia's Double Staggered Screens

Coach Larry Brown has used the following side out-of-bounds play to free Allen Iverson off two sets of staggered screens. The 2 (Iverson) sets up at the three-point line above the right elbow. He begins the play by making a Hawk-type cut off a high double stack of 4 and 5, who are aligned off the left elbow, shoulder to shoulder. The 2 moves to the left corner, and 1 cuts to the top off the first set of staggered screens from 5 and 4. The 3 inbounds to 1 (Eric Snow) and steps in. Positions

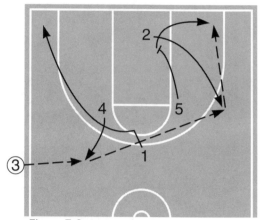

Figure 7.9.

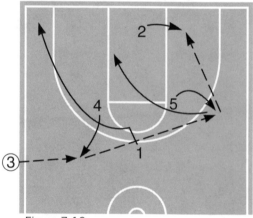

Figure 7.10.

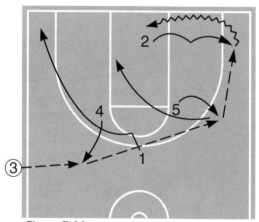

Figure 7.11.

4 and 5 now set a second set of staggered screens for 2, who cuts back to the right wing for the pass from 1. (See Fig. 7.12.)

Player 4 (Tyrone Hill) spots up toward the left corner, and 5 (Matt Geiger) holds at the left block as 2 begins his one-on-one move from his isolation position. Players 1 and 3 adjust their spot-up positions as 2 begins his penetration. (See Fig. 7.13.)

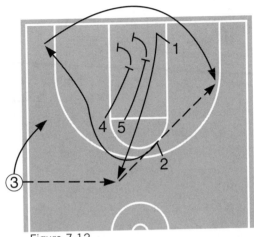

Figure 7.12.

Milwaukee Bucks' Triple Staggered Screens

Coach George Karl's crunch play sets up Ray Allen (3) for a three-point shot after he cuts off three screens. This action is run from a tight line off the left elbow. The alignment is 5-4-1-2, with 3 as the inbounder. The 1 pops out of the line for the pass from 3. At the same time, 2 begins his cut to the baseline. The 5 cuts into the lane to set the first screen of the triple staggers. Player 4 circles out toward the left wing to position himself so that he will set the last screen. It is important to have 4 (a big man) set the last screen because most teams will not switch a big man out to guard a 2. The 3 cuts inside of 4 to set the second screen. Player 2 cuts off the triple staggers set by 5, 3, and 4 for the pass from 1. (See Fig. 7.14.)

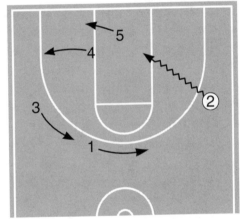

Figure 7.13.

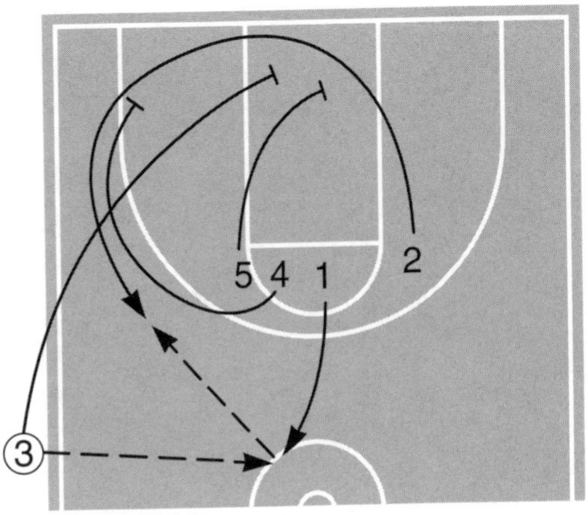

Minnesota's Box Set

Coach Flip Saunders uses an excellent misdirection action to free a shooter (in

Figure 7.14.

this case, Anthony Peeler) for a jump shot cutting off a double screen on the baseline. The play also builds in the possibility of a low post-feed to Kevin Garnett if the perimeter phase of the play is taken away by the defense. The play begins with 1 making a zipper cut to the top off a down screen from 5. Player 3 (Garnett) passes to 1 (Terrell Brandon), who runs a quick pick-and-roll with 4. Player 4 pops back after the pick-and-roll action. (See Fig. 7.15.)

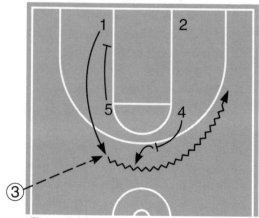

Figure 7.15.

The main thrust of the play is the misdirection action back to the weak side, but Brandon can look for his shot if he is open off the pick-and-roll. Position 1 begins the primary focus of the play with a pass to 4, who hits 2 cutting off the baseline staggered screens set by 5 and 3. The 2 looks for the jump shot as 5 clears out to the right block, with 3 posting up on the left block. Player 2 has the option of making the low post-feed to 3. If Garnett is open inside, Coach Saunders definitely encourages the 2 (Anthony Peeler) to get him the ball. (See Fig. 7.16.)

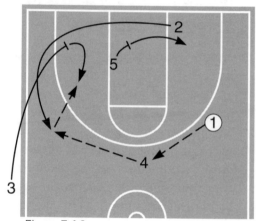

Figure 7.16.

CHAPTER 8

BASELINE OUT-OF-BOUNDS PLAYS

The following out-of-bounds plays are run with the ball taken out under the basket. They display actions used by teams to generate a quick score. They can be used during the normal course of the game but are very effective when run to free top players in the final seconds of a game.

Philadelphia '76ers' Baseline Stagger

Position 1 (Eric Snow) takes the ball out, with 2 (Allen Iverson) setting up on the opposite block and 3 (George Lynch) on the opposite elbow. Position 5 (Matt Geiger) starts on the ball-side block, with 4 (Theo Ratliff) on the ball-side elbow. The play begins with 2 setting a back screen on 3, who cuts hard to the basket. Obviously, if 3 is open

for a layup, 1 hits him. After setting the back screen, 2 cuts off 4 and 5, who step up to set staggered screens. The 1 looks to pass to 2 cutting off the screens for a jump shot. After setting the last screen, 5 slips to the rim and may be open if his defender helps on 2. (See Fig. 8.1.)

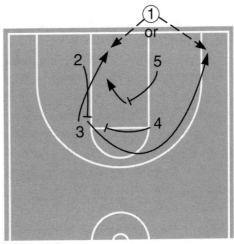

Figure 8.1.

Atlanta Hawks' Baseline Triple Stagger

During the 1998–99 season, Coach Lenny Wilkens set up a triple staggered screen play for Steve Smith for a three-point shot. Player 2 (Smith) is the inbounder, and 1 (Mookie Blaylock) begins at the ball-side block. Player 3 (Tyrone Corbin) aligns at the weak-side block, 4 (Alan Henderson) at the weak-side elbow, and 5 (Dikembe Mutombo) at the ball-side elbow. The 1 pops out to the corner for the inbounds pass. Player 2 hits 1 and cuts to the top off the triple staggered screens set by 3, 4, and 5. The 1 hits 2 for a possible three-point shot. (See Fig. 8.2.)

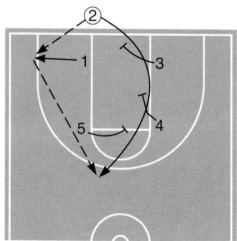

Figure 8.2.

Boston Celtics' Baseline Triple Stagger

This play from Coach Rick Pitino is run from a box set, with 3 (Adrian Griffin) serving as the inbounder. Position 2 (Paul Pierce) sets up on the weak-side block, and 1 (Dana Barros), who is the primary focus of the play, sets up at the weak-side elbow. The two big men begin on the ball-side of the floor, with 5 (Vitaly Potapenko) on the block and 4 (Antoine Walker) at the elbow. Player 5 pops out to the corner for the inbounds pass from 3. On the pass to 5, 4 sets a diagonal down screen for 2, who cuts to the top. The 5 passes to 2. (See Fig. 8.3a.)

The triple staggers begin with 3 stepping in to set the first screen for 1, who runs the baseline, also cutting off 4 and

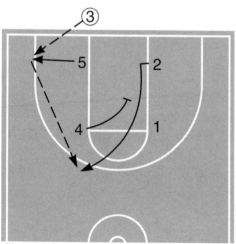

Figure 8.3a.

finally 5. Player 2 delivers the pass to 1 for the jump shot. (See Fig. 8.3b on page 80.)

Toronto Raptors' Baseline Zipper Play

The Raptors will run this baseline out-of-bounds play from a 1-4 set. The 3

Mookie Blaylock

(Vince Carter) is the inbounder with 1 (Alvin Williams), 4 (Charles Oakley), 2 (Doug Christie), and 5 (Kevin Willis) spread across the free-throw line extended. Players 1 and 4 serve to provide spacing and are not a part of this three-man play. Player 5 screens for 2, who cuts to the wing for the pass from 3. Position 5 now sets a second screen for 3, who zippers to the top. The 2 hits 3, who looks for the jump shot or for the one-on-one play. (See Fig. 8.4a.)

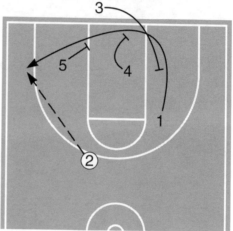

Figure 8.3b.

His teammates flatten out to the baseline, setting up a low 1-4 look to provide spacing for him to operate. (See Fig. 8.4b.)

Charlotte Hornets' Baseline Handoff Action

Coach Paul Silas's Hornets have won a game at the buzzer on this handoff action. Player 2 (Eddie Jones) is the inbounder, with the rest of the team aligned in a box set. Position 5 (Elden Campbell) is on the block directly in front of the ball, with 4 (Derrick Coleman) on the ball-side elbow. Position 3 (Anthony Mason) sets up on the opposite block, with 1 (David Wesley) at the elbow. This is a two-man play. Players 5 and 2 must work together to pull this play off successfully. The 5 must seal off his defender and free himself for the short inbounds pass, and 2 must decoy his man to free himself for a return pass. On the 2-to-5 pass, 4 screens for 1 at the top to occupy the defense, and 2 quickly cuts off 5 for the handoff and jump shot. (See Fig. 8.5.)

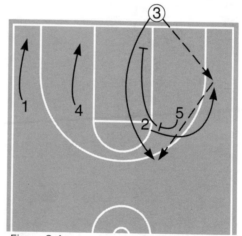

Figure 8.4a.

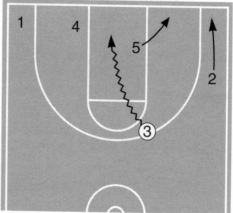

Figure 8.4b.

San Antonio Spurs' Baseline Short-Clock Play

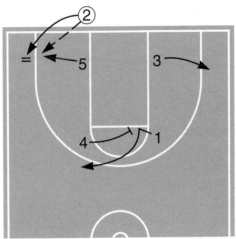

Figure 8.5.

With less than a second on the clock, Coach Gregg Popovich will set up a line play that has two options: (1) a lob to the rim for David Robinson or (2) a quick pop out for a jump shot for Sean Elliott. The 1 (Avery Johnson) is the inbounder. Players 5 (Robinson), 4 (Tim Duncan), and 3 (Elliott) position themselves in a tight line, with the last man set up at the elbow. Player 5 begins the play with an outside cut off 4 and 3 and a strong move to the front of the rim. Position 1 looks to throw the lob pass to 5 as the first option. As soon as 5 clears him, 3 cuts to the corner for a possible pass and quick jump shot. The 2 (Steve Kerr) begins at the opposite elbow and cuts deep to provide an additional passing option. (See Fig. 8.6.)

Cleveland Cavaliers' Baseline Out-Of-Bounds Plays

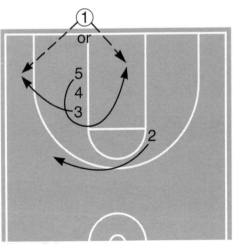

Figure 8.6.

Cleveland Cavalier Coach Randy Wittman has used the following baseline out-of-bounds plays to provide scoring action for Shawn Kemp and Bobby Sura.

The main thrust of the first play is the 4 spot. Player 3 (Lamond Murray) inbounds with 2 (Bobby Sura) and 5 (Andrew Declerq) in a stack in front of the ball. Player 1 (Andre Miller) sets up on the ball-side elbow and 4 (Shawn Kemp) is opposite 1. Player 2 pops to the corner and 5 dives hard to the opposite box looking for a pass. The 1 sets a screen for 4, who curls for the pass from 3. If the pass to 4 is denied,

3 can hit 2 in the corner. Position 2 reverses to 1 popping to the top, and 1 swing passes to 3 cutting off 5. (See Fig. 8.7.)

When the defense keys on the pass to 4, Coach Wittman runs the following counter. Position 2 pops to the corner, and 5 dives across the lane. The 1 still sets the screen on 4, but instead of cutting for the pass, 4 sets a back screen on 2, who flares for the pass from 3. This results in a jump shot for Sura. If this pass is denied, 3 looks to 1, cutting to the left baseline off a back screen from 5. The Murray-to-Miller pass is an excellent secondary scoring option. (See Fig. 8.8.)

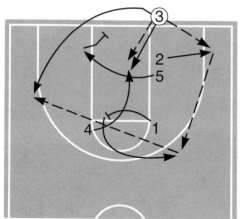

Figure 8.7.

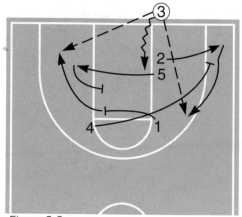

Figure 8.8.